Praise for the Book

'Increased participation of women in the Indian workforce is an economic and social imperative. This book encourages young women to think big by showing them success stories of relatable role models from diverse professions and backgrounds. Varsha's book is a must-read for all Indian girls and women. I highly recommend it!'
— **Akshay Kothari, Head of International, LinkedIn**

'There has never been a more exciting time for this book – women are forging a new path forward, and these personal stories from India's pioneering young women will spark the motivation needed for the next generation of change. These stories powerfully highlight the modern Indian woman's important role as a change-maker, boundary-breaker and shaper of her own destiny.'
— **Rachana Bhide, Bloomberg**

'*Wonder Girls* is an inspiring set of stories about possibilities that one can relate to – real-life stories about young women achieving success the way they define it. I would gift this book to my daughter. Thanks to Varsha for coming up with this wonderful book, and thanks to each of the women featured for sharing her incredible journey . . . truly inspirational!'
— **Muthiah Venkateswaran, Consultant, Spencer Stuart**

'The stories of role models showcased in this book offer confidence and direction to young women to pursue their dreams. The book highlights in exquisite detail the strength and fortitude with which women overcome the challenges that come their way. A truly inspirational read!'
— **Priya Naik, Founder & CEO, Samhita Social Ventures**

'I wish *Wonder Girls* existed when I was growing up! It would have made me realize sooner that I had it in me to follow my dreams.'
— **Kaneez Surka, Improv artist and stand-up comic**

'The attributes of a successful leader in our world today – compassion, creativity and intelligence – are not gendered. These stories in *Wonder Girls* will empower young women to tap into their immense potential, unconstrained by the expectations of others. If you can see it, or read about it, you can be it!'

Lavanya Ashok, Goldman Sachs

Wonder Girls

Wonder Girls

Success Stories of Millennials Who Fought to Do It Their Way

Varsha Adusumilli

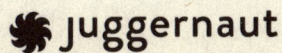

JUGGERNAUT BOOKS
KS House, 118 Shahpur Jat, New Delhi 110049, India

First published by Juggernaut Books 2018

Copyright © Varsha Adusumilli 2018

10 9 8 7 6 5 4 3 2 1

The views and opinions expressed in this book are the author's own. The facts contained herein were reported to be true as on the date of publication by the author to the publishers of the book, and the publishers are not in any way liable for their accuracy or veracity.

ISBN 9789386228802

All rights reserved. No part of this publication may be reproduced, transmitted, or stored in a retrieval system in any form or by any means without the written permission of the publisher.

Typeset in Adobe Caslon Pro by R. Ajith Kumar, New Delhi

Printed at Manipal Technologies Limited

To my grandfather
Dr Mandava Venkata Krishna Rao

Contents

Foreword by Vani Kola   xi

Introduction   1
1. Rugby Captain: Neha Pardeshi   5
2. Neurosurgeon: Vasundhara Rangan   23
3. CEO and Fitness Coach: Nilparna Sen   39
4. Artist: Shilo Shiv Suleman   55
5. Physics Professor: Prerna Sharma   71
6. Flight Commander: Rucha Nirale   89
7. Brand Marketer: Ruth Sequeira   105
8. Photographer: Shravya Kag   117
9. Scientist: Nishma Dahal   135
10. Casting Director: Shoumie Mukherjee   151
11. Actress: Shweta Tripathi   165
12. Radio Jockey: Sucharita Tyagi   179

13. Rock Climber: Gowri Varanashi — 195
14. Classical Dancer: Priyanka Chandrasekhar — 209
15. Visual Artist: Rhea Gupte — 223

Success Mantras — 239
Exercise for Readers — 245
References — 247
Acknowledgements — 253
A Note on the Author — 256

Foreword

A river always flows to its full potential despite the diversions and resistances along the way

A role model challenges your limitations, opens up new horizons and inspires you to become something more than what you may have expected of yourself. In understanding the lives and choices of your role models, valuable insights unfold, offering lessons that help you make your own choices.

As I look back on my life, I see three strong women as my role models. My mother, who was a pillar of conviction, believed that education for my sister and me was the highest priority for the family. My Telugu teacher, who cultivated in me an appreciation for poetry, taught me critical analysis techniques that could be applied to any topic. She also encouraged me to participate in debates and stand up for myself confidently. These skills have truly served me throughout my life and career. My third role model was my maths teacher, who refused to accept my failures and, in nurturing my intellect, showed me that with hard work and the right attitude, I could make it to the top. Truly unlocking someone's hidden potential is probably the best thing role models do.

A little later in life, my role models turned out to be people whom I didn't know intimately, but whose lives reflected a kind of success that could not have been predicted, given their earlier life circumstances. By reading about such people and by meeting some of them, I derived the courage to dream big and try things that were beyond my immediate reach or beyond the circumstances of my birth. At every phase of life, I looked for role models from whom I could get the answers I wanted for the path I had chosen. A role model's journey serves as an inspiration to forge ahead on one's own chosen path as it gets harder.

One of the questions I was often asked in the mid-1980s, when I moved to the US, was: 'Are Indian women more like you, or are you unlike most Indian women?' Perhaps this question was prompted by my enthusiasm and curiosity to try out things unfamiliar to me, like hiking down the Grand Canyon, learning to swim long distance, cross-country skiing, etc. Truly speaking, I never felt that I was unique. I always felt that Indian women are extremely strong and that they showcase their strength in different ways. Even though my mother had a limited education, she was strong for her children; it is her strength that I have inherited. Today my strength is perhaps better recognized than my mother's – or many an Indian woman's – ever was. But I know that my mother had the strength to accomplish the things that mattered to her and that she faced many challenges with faith and courage.

The heritage of Indian women is their quiet strength, which they pass on to the next generation of daughters. The need of the hour is that we give our daughters the scope to pursue the path that calls to them. I hope we don't pull them back into a prison where their dreams and aspirations are curtailed in the name of safety or tradition.

When Varsha asked me to write the foreword for this book, I immediately said yes, as the cause of showcasing role models whose lives other young women can relate to resonated deeply with me. Common to all the young women featured in this book is a set of core traits I admire. These traits were also what got me to notice Varsha in 2011, when she was working at a digital media start-up, YourStory. I could immediately see a young woman who cared about excellence, who was deeply committed to her work, was extremely smart, confident and fearless, and was marching to her own drumbeat. I saw someone who would create an impact on others through her life, and I kept tabs on her, staying in touch with her. Over time, my relationship with Varsha evolved as we worked on many projects together. Each time we worked on a project, she brought in the same level of consistency, focus, energy and commitment to excellence, and a deep thirst to learn. When she was switching careers, I asked her to work on a new initiative I wanted to start at Kalaari Capital, called Kstart. Varsha worked with me for two years, and in her highly effective way played an instrumental role in setting up Kstart, our seed initiative. As the time came for her to pursue other passions, I was glad to support her, and now I am excited be part of this book. Varsha plays an important role in bringing out the voice of a particular generation – and that voice is really one of the modern Indian woman who is strong, confident and wants to live life without compromising her dreams.

Though the intent of this book is to reach out to young women and unlock their potential and aspirations, I would also recommend this book to partners, parents and friends of those young women, which is basically all of us. This book explains the pulse of India through what Indian women of today represent.

As a river flows, it encounters many diversions and much resistance, yet one thing about the river is immutable: drawn by its natural force, it always finds a way into the ocean to renew the cycle of life. In India, the river is always considered feminine. It represents strength and power, and is famed both for its giving attitude and for achieving its objective. By reading this book, I hope every reader, just like the river, finds the courage to fuel her own passions and flow onwards to fulfil her potential, giving back to the world and enriching the lives she touches along the way.

I hope you enjoy as much as I did the stories of the courageous young women in this book.

Vani Kola, MD, Kalaari Capital

Introduction

In 2016, I attended my best friend's wedding in Jaipur. Little did I know that it would be a life-altering occasion for me. The wedding was spread out over a few days, and during my time there I met many young local girls who were brimming with enthusiasm and questions. Once I befriended the girls and they were comfortable in my presence they began to open up to me about the issues that deeply mattered to them. But first I had to answer the many questions they were looking for answers to.

'Didi, how old are you?' 'Why are you still unmarried?' 'Aren't your parents worried that you're not married?' 'You've travelled abroad?! How?' 'Your parents allow you to live alone?' 'Didi, I want to get a job in the city. How can I do this?' 'Didi, I really want to become a doctor. How can I convince my parents?'

I was intrigued to see that their questions followed a similar and predictable track, and this set me thinking. As I told them my life story, I noticed a spark in their eyes as they discovered that there were many life and career choices that existed in the world. The girls were genuinely happy to find someone they could relate to, someone who was also slightly unconventional. In that moment of their discovery and comfort, I had inadvertently sparked a desire in their young minds – that they too could pursue their own unique paths. Exposing these young girls to new choices felt like breathing new life into their beings.

It was clear to me that these young girls were seeking role models they could look up to and consult while making important life decisions. Magazines, journals and newspapers obsessively focus on women achievers, which is necessary and important too, but the women featured by them are too far ahead in their journeys, and many regular Indian girls cannot relate to them. Regular Indian girls crave stories of initiative from their next-door neighbours, someone who speaks their language, someone who dresses like them and someone they could, perhaps, have access to.

Once I was back from the wedding, I began researching women and their careers, and the data I acquired was surprising. Only 27 per cent of working-age women have jobs in India.[1] In China, this figure is 61 per cent, while in the United States it is 56 per cent.[2] Even though the employment rates for women are growing the world over, in India those numbers are sliding.[3] Yes, women are getting educated in huge numbers, but that is not necessarily translating into workforce participation.[4] This is a problem that needs solving.

Several ongoing and past researches indicate that when women work outside their homes there is better decision-making at home, which leads to healthier families overall. Encouraging participation of women in the workforce is not only a social but also an economic imperative. According to a Mckinsey report published in 2015, India would add a whopping $700 billion to its GDP in 2025 if women's workforce participation advanced towards equality with that of men.[5]

As the adage goes, 'If she can see it, she can become it.' I want to show young Indian women that there are many different career options for them in the world. They can be anything and do anything they set their hearts and minds on. The stories in this book peek into the lives of young women who have pursued and excelled in many diverse careers, and whom the regular Indian girl can relate to. The women featured in this book range from scientists to artists, from neurosurgeons to sportspersons. And they've all had to cross many hurdles to achieve their goals. This book is an attempt to bridge the role model gap for Indian girls. Choosing your own career is not easy as there is usually immense parental and societal pressure to do as others want you to. But, as you will find out after reading this book, choosing your own path is the most satisfying and sometimes the only option that makes sense.

When my publisher and I were working on shaping the chapters, we were shocked by the minuscule percentage of female workforce participation in many Indian industries.

If 27 per cent is the best that we can achieve, then we have miles to go before we sleep. According to an article written by Rohini Pande and Charity Troyer Moore in *The New York Times*, all is not doom and gloom.[6] The good news is that when conditions are favourable, Indian women have made significant strides in the workplace. Women head large banks in India. Twelve per cent of the pilots employed by Indian airlines are women.[7] This is a favourable statistic, against the worldwide average of 5 per cent.

Women can be each other's guides and inspiration. If you are a woman in the professional workforce, find a young girl in your community and tell her about your work and why you do what you do. Seek out other girls and share your passion with them. If you are a young woman interested in finding a role model you can relate to, ask the people in your network, research online, reach out to the role models you find and nudge them to tell you their secrets. Create a giant network of women, each supporting the next, and let the chain be infinite. Every little step is one big stride in empowering women.

This book is a step towards getting more women into India's workforce – and not just in traditional careers. I sincerely hope this book inspires young women to choose their own career paths and model their lives as they would like them to be. My hope is that when we show young women relatable role models they will gain the courage to take a leap of faith. I want young women to read this book and think – if they can do it, so can I!

1

Rugby Captain: Neha Pardeshi

Only one per cent of Indian girls have played any kind of organized sport in their lives[8]

I am of small build. But that has never stopped me from doing what I do.

When I tell people that I'm a rugby player, they look at me in disbelief and shock. 'It can't be,' they say. 'You are so tiny!' 'How do you play this beast of a sport?' 'Is this a joke?' I laugh their comments away, because you really have to see me in action to know how strong I actually am.

But why rugby? Have you lost your mind? – you may ask. Why not cricket, or tennis, or badminton?

Here's why: I found rugby when I was fifteen and I fell in love with it.

I am a young middle-class woman from Pune. I was the first girl from my family who went to an English-medium school; all my cousins studied in Marathi-medium schools. My parents had to fight my paternal grandparents to enrol me in an English-medium school. My grandparents believed that kids who go to English-medium schools are not well mannered. They feared I would turn out to be a brat. My earliest memory of my schooldays is of shifting back and forth between English- and Marathi-medium schools. My mother was relentless about her insistence on an English-medium school for me, and eventually she won my grandparents over. The school I was finally admitted to gave equal importance to academics, arts and sports.

My mother and father ran a small gym in our locality. My father used to take me to gymnastics class every evening when I was in class one. He noticed that I was doing well in that sport, so he pushed me to train at any opportunity I got. My father loved sports. In fact, he was into bodybuilding when he was younger.

The Pune racecourse was located very close to my school. My father would take me to the racecourse every morning before he dropped me off at school. I loved running on the race track. I still remember how happy that morning ritual of ours made me feel. By the time I got to class three I was the fastest runner at school, winning all the competitions. I would challenge anyone who was willing to race with me, and I don't remember ever losing.

One day, the handball coach at school noticed me running during one of the physical education classes and asked me to give the sport a try. I did. I was ten years old at the time.

I began training with my handball coach every day. I would also do the practice drills all by myself, before and after school hours. My father would take me to school an hour early and pick me up an hour after school. Making a mark in sports is excruciatingly hard, but my parents' emotional support was critical in my journey.

I participated in handball selections several times at the state level but, unfortunately, I lost out to less competent players every time. I never understood why I was losing. Back home, I would cry, as I was devastated every time I was not picked. I knew I was the best player that showed up for the selections, but why was I not making the cut? Was there something wrong with me? Was I not doing enough work? I would convince myself that if I worked harder I would make it the next year. I would ask the coaches to help me out in my weaker areas. I would train like crazy. I once did 200 dodges in one session. My coach thought I was going nuts. My tryst with handball continued for four years. Every year I would work insanely hard, but the outcome never changed. I never made it past the state-level selections in handball.

I was thirteen when I figured out that the person who got selected every time was the daughter of the tournament sponsor. That was my first brush with the dirty politics of the sporting world. I had to learn to come to terms with it.

My dejection with handball was so apparent that it came to the notice of the school athletics coach, who asked me to try out the track. Having given up all hope in handball, I threw myself into athletics with determination. It was athletics that led me to participate at the national level, in the category of hurdles. I trained hard for it, waking early every morning to run across the city. I am familiar with every nook and corner of Pune because I would run a different route every morning.

Athletes are addicted to competition, winning and getting ahead. In the beginning, I was desperate to play at the state level. My prayer in those days was simple, 'God, please give me an opportunity to play for my state.' Eventually, when I got to play at the national level, I was hungry to represent the country in international tournaments. When I showed up for the national-level hurdle races, they were also selecting teams for the Commonwealth Games. I thought I was going to make the cut, but I tripped during the selections. The girl who was behind me was selected instead. I felt humiliated. I cried for days, like a sore loser. My mother would often say, 'You are my daughter. You are not a loser. You will find a way. Keep going.'

My failure only egged me on further, and a new dream took hold – I wanted to play for my country. Gradually, this dream became an obsession.

Of course, alongside all of this I had to study too. I was not a stellar student, but that didn't mean I ignored my studies. I did reasonably well at school and college. I didn't fail any exams. After college, I got a job as a digital and outdoor marketer at a Pune firm. Even though sports was my first love, I had to make a living.

During my stint in athletics, I accidentally got introduced to rugby via a local club in Pune. Coach Surhud Khare from the Khare Football and Rugby Academy, Pune, visited our school and invited us to attend the women's rugby match that he was organizing over the weekend. One of my friends and I went to watch the match, just for fun. We enjoyed the game so much that we wanted to give it a try. Surhud encouraged us to attend a practice session. He had grown up in Africa and had played rugby all through his childhood. When he came back to India he made a commitment to introduce and grow rugby in India. Surhud is the reason why people play rugby in Pune today. He introduced the local football players to rugby, and they passionately took to the new sport. Surhud later confessed to me that he didn't think I had it in me to be a rugby player. 'You are so small. I never thought you could play this sport. I changed my mind after I saw you run. Any doubts I had were wiped out after I saw you tackle your opponents.'

That one practice session changed my life forever. I had played nearly every sport there was, but had never enjoyed any of them as much as I did rugby. There was no looking back after that evening.

I was fifteen at the time. Since then I have been showing up for my rugby practice session from 6 a.m. to 8 a.m. every single day. I played rugby in the scorching heat and during the harsh monsoon. I made no excuses. The only days I skip are when I am out of Pune for a tournament.

'Why do you love rugby so much?' a friend once asked me. 'You have played other sports before, but why this?'

Most people think rugby is a sport for hooligans. The truth is far from it. Every rugby player I know is extremely kind and respectful. What draws me to rugby are the core values the sport inculcates in its players. I can tell you that my life after rugby has been very different from my life before it. The sport of rugby revolves around solidarity, respect, integrity, discipline and fairness. Coach Surhud taught me how to inculcate these core values in my game. I have seen men who are seven feet tall and weighing over 100 kg play the sport like beasts, but off the field they are true gentlemen.

A few years ago, I was going through a rough phase because of a financial situation at home. I told nobody about it, but my teammates could sense that something was not quite right with me. Throughout that phase my teammates constantly checked in on me. They would visit me often and WhatsApp me stupid jokes to make me laugh. They sensed my unsaid problems in a way that only sportspersons can.

Sports also taught me confidence. Rugby involves tackling opponents. It's a different kind of confidence-builder to knock down a giant opponent with just shrewdness or deftness of technique. I have done thousands of tackles so far. Since I am small of build no one expects me to tackle and bring down bigger opponents, but I always do. Sometimes you get tackled and fall too. The rule of rugby is to get back on your feet and dive back into the thick of it. Because of rugby, I know that no matter what challenges life may throw at me, I can tackle them . . . and even if I fall, what's the worst thing that could happen? I will get back up and keep going. This spirit is deeply ingrained in me now.

My commitment to and consistency with rugby paid

off. In early 2016, I was made captain of the Indian rugby team. I cried when I heard the news. I didn't know what to do. I called up my father, crying, and he thought I was in trouble. He began to freak out. '*Beta, kya hua? Kya hua?*' he kept asking. When I was finally able to stop crying I told him I had been made captain of the Indian rugby team and didn't know what to do. My father burst out laughing. He told me I fully deserved the title.

A few months before the Asian 7s tournament in 2016, I suffered a debilitating injury. My situation was grim: people who had seen how badly injured I was just a few months prior to the big tournament didn't think I had any chance of representing India at the Asian 7s, let alone captaining the team.

It was October 2016. The rugby nationals in Odisha were coming up in three months. I had grown overconfident and wanted to push myself with my training. One evening, I was working out at my mother's gym and I ended up doing twenty repetitions of 90 kg deadlifts. That's a hell of a lot of weight to lift!

When I got back home that night from the gym my back was extremely sore from the intensive exercise, but I brushed it aside. Injury in sports is a natural price a sportsperson has to pay. No pain, no gain. I was accustomed to soreness. I thought my back would heal soon so I wasn't worried. I had my high-protein dinner, reviewed my daily task list, wrote the day's journal entry and played with my cats before going to bed.

The next day I woke up at 5 a.m., went for a run and,

later, for my 6 a.m. rugby practice session. It was business as usual. During practice I strained my back after passing the ball. The pain was excruciating. I could not stand up straight, bend down or even touch my toes. I was operating like a robot. I would wake up in the middle of the night and cry uncontrollably.

When I finally went to see a doctor, he took one look at my anxious face and said, 'Don't even think about the upcoming tournament. There is absolutely no way you will be able to play, let alone compete fiercely at a rugby tournament.' My back was injured and the muscles were severely knotted up.

The doctor tried needle therapy on my back and glutes for the next couple of days. He was working through the knots day after day, but there was no relief. I figured his treatment was not going to help me. I had a tournament coming up and I needed to get better. So I decided to try something else.

I reached out to an acquaintance who was a physiotherapist. After she examined me she said, 'Don't get your hopes up too much. There is a small chance that you might get better before the tournament. If you want that to happen, you will have to visit me every day for the therapy sessions, and you will have to strictly follow my instructions.'

Her facility was a forty-five-minute drive from my home, which didn't deter me at all, as not playing the nationals was not an option for me. I was determined to fix my back.

The months leading up to the tournament were some of the hardest I've had to endure. I continued to wake up at 5 a.m., followed my training regimen, showed up at my day job, and after work drove my scooter to the physiotherapist's by late evening. It would be 11 p.m. by the time I got home. The therapy was a far-from-pleasant experience. In fact, saying that the process was painful would be an understatement. At one point I had twenty-seven needles in my back for fifteen minutes! It was horrible. If I ever have to picture what hell looks like, I just have to think about that one therapy session. But I needed to recover. I had no choice. And, on top of the physical pain came the financial burden too. I was paying through my nose for the sessions.

And that's another thing I've lived with all my life.

To this day rugby hasn't paid me, but I have never been bitter about it. I was always fully aware that in India, unless you played cricket or badminton, you can't really make a living by being a sportsperson. It was with this in mind that all through my college years, while I was pursuing the sport seriously, I made sure my studies never suffered. Later, I knew I had to keep my day job if I wanted to continue my passion for rugby. Otherwise my dream wouldn't be possible, and I would be on the road.

My mother confronted me during my injury phase, concerned with the rising doctor's bills. 'What are you doing? Rugby is not going to pay you anything. What do you think you will become eventually? Where do you think you are headed in life?'

I couldn't tell her that there would come a time when my passion would sustain me financially, because that's the honest truth. But I did convince her that rugby is where my heart lies. Even if there is no money in it, it's fine, I told her. I will have to keep playing to maintain my sanity, even if that meant I had to work two jobs every day. My mother has largely been supportive and understanding, but there are phases when she worries about what will happen to me. As a parent, her anxiety is justifiable.

Two weeks into the physiotherapy, I could finally bend down to pick up a pencil from the ground. I was making progress, but slowly. Within a month, my range of motion improved slightly. My mother saw how disciplined I was all through this phase. She finally realized that I was not going to give up on my dream, come what may. She came to terms with my passion for rugby and began to encourage me. 'Keep going, Neha! Don't overthink this. Follow the exercises and the routine. You will be fine.' Her reassurance and presence were crucial in my recovery. Sometimes, psychological assurance is all one needs not to break.

My injury happened in October 2016, leaving me with November and December for recovery before the nationals began. Following the nationals, we were scheduled to play at the Asian 7s in Laos in February. The nationals were being held in Odisha. Two weeks prior to the nationals, I was able to run. I felt ready to play again.

My efforts had paid off. Nobody had thought I would recover, but with the right help and guidance I recovered and played the nationals. Of course, I was nervous about the games. The fear of injuring my back again haunted me. I had just come out of a terrible injury. Was I strong enough? Could I do it? What if it exacerbated the injury? What if I wound up on the therapy table once again? I couldn't afford the expense involved. It would be all over for me.

Fear is the biggest killer on a rugby field. Rugby is a brutal sport. I had to flush any fear and apprehension I had out of my system. Athletes are masters at self-talk. We know how to trick our minds and talk ourselves into things we want to believe. I repeatedly told myself that if I was perpetually scared of getting back on the field, I would definitely get injured, but if I did not allow myself to get scared and let myself be, there was a good chance that I wouldn't get injured again at all. Let fear go. Let fear go. Let fear go. I hung on to this mantra as if it were a lifeline.

And then, something magical happened on the day of the match. I stepped out onto the field to play, and at once all my anxiety, fear and apprehension disappeared. This was rugby, and I knew what I had to do with my eyes closed. What had I been worried about all this time? I had worked hard towards it, driven my body through hell and back, and there was nothing stopping me now. My concentration on the ball kicked in. It was the only thing I could see. And this is why I never gave up rugby. It makes me singularly focused, to the point where my mind is a blank slate; it frees me from fear and gives me a kind of freedom I can never describe. When I am on the field, it's as if I am transported into a different world. Nothing bothers me any more. Rugby has been my form of meditation.

I successfully completed the national tournament. Our team came second, and that was amazing because I had overcome my pain and fear and played the complete tournament without missing a single match. It was an exhilarating experience.

Next up was the Asian 7s tournament. The team had a three-day break between the nationals and training, which was going to be held in Mumbai. The practice sessions were rigorous. Our days were broken up into three parts – mornings for fitness, afternoons for half-time fitness and skills, and evenings for the brutal, three-hour-long, straight-up rugby skill session. By the end of day, we were bone-tired, and all we could think of was sleep. And, on top of all this I was putting in a little extra session for myself. Before every session, I would do my back and core exercises. I would also tape my back up for extra strength. This was the phase when I had the maximum injuries ever as a player. I was on painkillers every day.

It was critical for team India to win the Asian 7s. I had to perform. As a captain, you have to lead by example. You can't make excuses and back out. I don't believe in commanding people and telling them what to do. It was taken for granted that everyone on the team knew how to play; my responsibility was to inspire my team and to rise to the occasion. When selection day came, I was among the twelve women who were going to play the Asian 7s in Laos. The news reported my captaincy. I was thrilled with the outcome and proud that I hadn't given up. My dream of playing for my country had been realized.

We came back home from Laos with a silver medal. Gold would have been great, but I was happy we had secured second place and that we'd put rugby on the sporting map of India. Coming back home after the Asian 7s was exhilarating, and I enjoyed every moment of it. My parents were bombarded with calls from friends and family sending in their wishes. It was the first time I knew with absolute surety that I'd made them proud.

Prime Minister Modi announced our achievement on radio, congratulating Indian women for winning a medal. Before this, very few people knew I played rugby, and there was little to no awareness about the sport. But our win at Laos changed all that. Before Laos, most people didn't even know a sport called rugby was played in India, and the fact that girls also played this sport was shocking to them. Women's rugby has so much potential. Any investment in girls is good for the country. I never expected the Asian 7s win to generate so much of a buzz around rugby.

Many people reached out to me after this tournament. It was the first time I had received any recognition for the sport I loved so much. After this tournament, I was paid Rs 25,000 by the Indian Rugby Football Union. For the first time in nine years since I picked up the sport, I had earned something through the sport I loved so much.

As a sportsperson playing for the country, it is

embarrassing to scramble so much for resources. Will I continue to play this sport?

My answer is a resounding yes. I will play rugby even if there is no fame or money involved. Rugby is what makes me come alive. I play the sport because I want to. Most people who play this sport get nothing out of it, but they do it because they truly love it. I don't mind the expenses or the sheer toughness of it all. In all these years, I have not thought even once about switching to badminton or something else because it'll be more lucrative. I know I could switch sports if I wanted to, but I won't. And I am grateful for my parents' support. How many Indian parents will encourage their child to take up something that gives her no financial return?

The life I've chosen is fraught with difficulties and hurdles. My father knows what rugby means to me, and I can do what I do only because I have his support 100 per cent. This kind of unfailing love gives me the confidence to face each day as it comes. And my life is far from a bed of roses. On most days I struggle to balance my job alongside my practice sessions and travel commitments for the tournaments. But I've made my peace with it because this is the path I've chosen. Without my day job, it would be hard to make ends meet. Also, I learn from being a marketer. I am thankful to my boss, who is also active in the Pune rugby clubs. He too is passionate about rugby, so he understands the demands of the sport and keeps work flexible for me. He understands that rugby is my priority.

Eventually, I want to start a sporting goods company. I strongly believe that everything I do is leading me towards that goal, because I learn from everything I do. There are days when I get depressed. Why am I working so hard? Should I be doing this? But then I reason with myself – how many people truly find their calling or have the courage to go against the odds to pursue what they love?

It would have been great to have a full-time career in sports, but India is not there yet, though I can sense that we will get there in the future.

My persistence is beginning to pay off. After the Asian 7s, I received a few sponsorship opportunities and bagged some local advertising gigs with fitness brands. Now I get invited by various organizations to coach children, which I occasionally do over the weekends. And in 2018, we are privileged to be representing India at the Asian Games in Jakarta.

When I played rugby for the first time the Indian women's rugby team didn't even exist. There were local enthusiasts' clubs in cities such as Mumbai, Kolkata and Pune. I was part of the very first Indian national rugby team when it was founded in 2009. It took seven years of persistent training for me to become captain of the Indian team and win the Asian 7s medal.

The future of rugby is bright. Today rugby is the fastest growing sport in India, and that is because of passionate leaders like Suhrud who go from school to school introducing rugby to young people. It takes an immense amount of passion to show up every morning for ten years at 6 a.m. to coach beginners. Players like me owe everything to coaches like him.

There is a strong girls' rugby team in a place as remote as Siliguri today. Who would have thought that, right? At the Pune local club, though, it's been very hard to recruit girls to play the sport. Only 1 per cent of Indian girls have played any kind of organized sport. And, in addition to all these constraints, rugby has a problem in the way it is perceived too.

Things are changing, albeit very slowly. I have had a few mothers who have asked me to coach their girls. Today, when I coach young girls, I try to ingrain the values of rugby in them the way my coaches did in me. Some of the parents have come back to me to ask, 'What have you done for my child? She is so disciplined now. She is so confident. She has been optimistic lately. She is not rude to anybody any more.' The things you learn on the field stay with you off the field. My goal is to popularize rugby and the values of the game in India, especially among women.

Nasser Hussain, who is the head coach of the Indian Rugby Football Union, plays a key role in taking rugby to grassroots India. Nasser used to be an incredible player. Post retirement, he dedicated his life to rugby. He spends every waking moment of his life pushing rugby and coaching players to achieve more. I'll never forget his words to me during the Asian 7s, 'You need to make a difference.' And that is what I strive to do every single waking minute of my life.

2

Neurosurgeon: Vasundhara Rangan

There are less than 100 women
neurosurgeons in India[9]

'My wish is for Vasundhara to become a doctor,' my father said, lying on his hospital bed just a few months before he passed away.

By then he was bald, lanky and physically drained. The cancer and chemotherapy had taken a toll on him. This was in 1993, and I was seven years old. Even though that memory is now a blur, it is a defining part of my identity.

I was too young to understand what my father was going through when he was battling cancer. All I knew was that he was going to die soon. My mother fiercely protected my sister and me during this phase. We were kept too busy with school, tuitions and homework to comprehend the graveness of it all.

My parents' marriage had been an arranged one. They had a typical Tamil Brahmin wedding. My mother was nineteen when she got married; she had me at twenty and my sister at twenty-three. My father was swiftly climbing the corporate ladder as a marketing professional at Lipton in Chennai. He was making excellent money and had bought a car when he was just twenty-five. Buying a car was a big deal for working-class people back in those days. My parents had built a wonderful little life together. My mother worked in a bank. She wanted to quit her job to take care of us children full-time, but my father, as if he could predict the future, never let her do so.

It was when my father began looking for a house to buy in Chennai that he was diagnosed with cancer. My mother was devastated. Life as she knew it collapsed. Father's cancer changed our lives forever. The regular hospital visits, the medication and the treatment costs rapidly changed our financial situation. Hospitalization for a chronic condition can reduce a patient and family to nothing. I learned this lesson very early on in my life. After leading a comfortable upper-middle-class life, my family was now struggling to make ends meet. Suddenly, we couldn't afford to buy vegetables any more. My mother reminds me of a time when I asked for French beans and she couldn't buy them because they were priced at Rs 30 a kg. All she had with her was Rs 5 when she went to the local vegetable market, so she returned home with spinach, which cost Rs 3 then. From having a cook, a driver, a gardener and a full-time caretaker at home, we ended up as a family with no household help. People who know our story often ask me about how I coped with those sudden changes as a child. The answer to that question lies in my mother's resourcefulness. I think we ate many innovative variations of spinach and dal in those days.

My father passed away a few months after my

seventh birthday. We moved to Hyderabad immediately afterwards because our maternal grandparents lived there, and we needed their emotional support. In Chennai, we had lived in a bungalow. In Hyderabad, we moved into a one-bedroom apartment. My father's death changed my mother's life completely. At twenty-seven, my mother had to start her life all over from scratch. My mother had been protected all through her childhood by my grandparents, and then by my father, who had adored her. Because of an accident of fate, she went from being someone who had never had to worry about anything to having to worry about making ends meet and raising two kids all by herself. As a single mother, she had to face a whole new set of problems. Our paternal grandmother, who had lived with us in Chennai, moved to Hyderabad, along with us. My mother was now a working single parent. And having my paternal grandmother at home and my maternal grandparents around the corner was helpful; my paternal grandmother took care of us when my mother went to work.

Our next-door neighbours were wealthy. However, my mother never allowed us to feel that we didn't have enough. She sent us to a good school in Hyderabad and enrolled us in any extracurriculars that our money could buy. We had enough good food to eat at home. Sure, we didn't have access to a swimming pool and didn't do fancy vacations, but somehow that didn't bother us. At the back of our minds, my sister and I knew that my mother was already giving us the best she could, and we never really asked for or wanted anything more than what we had. Homework, tuitions, dance and music classes kept us occupied.

All through my years at school, I was fully aware of how hard my mother worked to make ends meet. I took responsibility for my studies because I never wanted to let her down. I consistently excelled in coursework. My upbringing was typically Tamil Brahmin. After school, veena lessons and Kuchipudi training were serious business. I cleared my music and dance exams. Heck, I even acted in a Telugu movie when I was in class five. The movie was directed by a famous Telugu director, and was an adaptation of the Ramayana, but with children as the primary cast. The director and his crew went from school to school in Hyderabad auditioning kids. The director would later tell me that the very moment he saw me, he knew he wanted to cast me as Kaikeyi. My family would have never agreed to let me act in a movie, but for them there is no god holier than Lord Ram. The moment they heard the movie was based on the Ramayana, they couldn't say no!

This movie turned out to be a launch pad for the Telugu movie superstar N.T. Rama Rao's grandson, and so it ended up eventually becoming a box-office blockbuster. They didn't pay us children anything for acting in the film, but this project was one of the most fun things I did growing up. I got to meet and hang out with children from many different schools in Hyderabad, and I became lifelong friends with some of them. We would finish shooting in the evening and play cards afterwards. My school allowed me to skip a few days, as I always topped in class.

After the film released, the cast went around in a truck to the interiors of Andhra Pradesh for movie promotions. The movie release was a big deal because of Junior NTR's launch. NTR fans mobbed us throughout the tour. People would throw garlands and flowers at us. I was a complete geek, and this was a hilarious experience for me. But when I realized how much time the movie took from my regular routine, I decided I never wanted to do movies again, even though I had received other film offers by then. I went back to my studies. I didn't let the temporary fame go to my head. I knew that all the garlands and cheers were for Junior NTR and not for me. I was smart enough to understand that even at that time. My core strength was academics. That was where I was able to excel, differentiate myself and truly shine.

My friends wondered how I managed both my studies and extracurriculars at the same time. I always had limited time to study after my dance and veena classes, so I had to be super focused during my study time. Whatever little I did for my studies, I did with interest and dedication. And so I balanced both aspects of my life. I knew that if I stopped all my extracurriculars and just studied, I would become hopelessly unproductive. I've seen many people who only focus on their work, but I'm not one of them. The more things I do, the more productive I am at all of those things. Some people are not meant to be superlatives in one field. They are meant to be good at a lot of things. I like doing many different things. Focus and perseverance are key to my being able to juggle various roles.

I decided to pursue medicine because I wanted to fulfil my dad's dream. I worked my butt off to secure admission into medical school. I secured an all-India rank of twenty-nine in the entrance exam to Manipal. I had mixed feelings about my rank. Manipal was prohibitively expensive, and I didn't want to make my mother pay for it, but she convinced me that it was ridiculous to think about money at that point. She told me that Manipal was a wonderful college for medicine, one of the best in the country, and that I should not let go of the opportunity. We could always take a loan and pay it off later. Since then, I have been to many other medical colleges, and in hindsight, joining Manipal was one of the best things I did for my career. That did not mean I didn't feel guilty that my mother and grandfather were repaying my education loan. I resolved to make it up to them in the future. I never asked for money from home for anything after graduating.

'Why send a girl away from home?'
'Is Manipal a safe place for girls?'
'Why spend that much money on daughters?'

My mother encountered all these questions and more from many of our relatives and neighbours. She was immune to such comments. She had endured hardship very early in life and it had made her thick-skinned to such comments. For my mother it didn't matter whether

I was a boy or a girl. I was her child, and I was extremely capable. I had proved myself consistently at school. Not for a moment did she doubt my decision to go to medical school.

People ask me how I made it this far despite having had a tumultuous childhood. And my answer always remains the same: I grew up surrounded by an eclectic mix of strong women who took care of me and sacrificed their immediate happiness for my future. My mother and both my grandmothers are madly different and fiercely independent. They have minds of their own and don't succumb to peer pressure. I grew up being influenced by them.

My mother accepted her first promotion after I moved to Berhampur for my postgraduation in general surgery. She had been offered promotions several times in the past. As a child I didn't understand why she kept turning them down because a promotion meant more money and hence a better life. One day I asked my mother why she had rejected the offers and she said, 'I would have had to move out of Hyderabad if I got promoted. I didn't want to rock the boat for you and your sister. I would like for you to have a stable childhood and access to a strong education.' She curtailed her career growth for us. This was just one of the many sacrifices my mother made for us. Marrying again was simply not an option that existed for her at the time.

I think all women have it in them to be extraordinary providers for their families. Many parents guilt-trip their children, expecting them to be grateful for everything they do for them. Not once did my mother ever bring up money in our discussions. I had been unlucky with my father's death, but I was richly compensated by my mother.

After Manipal, I was keen on pursuing surgery for my master's, but I was also determined to not have my mother pay for the postgraduate coaching classes. So, after wrapping up my undergrad work at Manipal, I moved to Delhi. This was a tactical decision on my part, because doctors are paid the best in Delhi. Coaching classes are expensive, and so I took up full-time work at a hospital in their neurosurgery department. I attended evening classes to prepare for the postgraduate entrance exams. The thing about medicine is that it is a long-drawn process, and one needs to work extremely hard and be singularly focused to clear any exams, but money is not much of a problem once you are through with it. It is highly unlikely that a well-trained doctor will ever be unemployed.

For my super specialization, I wanted to be closer to home. I wrote the entrance exams for a nationally reputed institute and was selected for the interview round. Only four out of the eight interview candidates were ultimately admitted. I had a nagging feeling that I wouldn't make it. And I was right. The college chose only men for the four available seats, even though, at the time, I felt I was highly qualified to secure admission. I even had practical experience in the field. I was devastated by their selection.

But I had to persist. Even though I wanted to be based in south India and was hoping to get into a school in Bengaluru, I sat for the entrance exam of the Postgraduate Institute of Medical Education and Research (PGIMER), Chandigarh. I thought the Chandigarh interview would be a good practice session. When the Chandigarh results were announced, I was stunned. I had come second nationwide. I knew PGIMER was one of the best medical schools in the country for neurosurgery. My family was in Hyderabad, and there I was, moving to Chandigarh. Geographically, it was an inconvenient arrangement, but I had no choice but to go ahead with it. When you get admission to PGIMER, you don't let it go.

During my residency in Chandigarh, I alternated between the ICU, the emergency wards and the operating theatre. I was at the hospital by 7.30 a.m. every morning. Every fifth day I was assigned to do the night shift, in which case my work began at 7 p.m. and ended at 9 a.m. the next morning. When there were surgeries planned, I did the required preparatory work – discussing the patient's case with the senior doctor performing the surgery. My job was to ensure that everything needed for the surgery was in place. There is no scope for error in our line of work. Pursuing medicine takes a toll on you. It's as if the catching up never ever ends. That is why doctors magically learn to fall asleep anywhere and at any time and, with similar ease, learn to pull consecutive all-nighters too.

Today I am a neurosurgeon; I finally fulfilled my father's last wish. As fancy as my job may seem, I must warn you, it is a very tough job. Surgery is like military training. If you are called at 3 a.m., you must wake up and show up. No excuses and no complaints. Every day is tough and full of surprises – and often, not the good kind. There is no set routine. The hospital shifts and work hours are crazy. Sometimes I have to stand for ten hours straight in an operating theatre. If you are someone who seeks work–life balance, surgery is the worst place to be in. Specialization in surgery in domains such as neuroscience is even more demanding. The specialization itself takes six years of studying and training. Most people are not willing to invest that kind of time.

I am almost always the only woman in a team of men in the operating room. And that is not a coincidence. In India, most women are expected to settle down by their late twenties – we are meant to get married, have kids and raise them. And so it is only logical that women do not consider surgery as a possible profession or are not allowed to do so.

There have been very few female neurosurgeons in India – less than one hundred women (across generations!). The current group is so small that most of us are connected with each other via one WhatsApp group!

Most women I know tell me they'd rather take up a normal nine-to-five job than do what I do. But it's sad when I hear girls tell me that they didn't even think surgery was an option available to them. Most women face this dilemma: what does she want to achieve by age thirty? Get married? Or be a doctor with no semblance of a social life? And let me tell you this, finding a life partner as a neurosurgeon can sometimes be harder than the job itself! Being a surgeon is a lonely career choice.

I was certain I had found the love of my life in college. He was stoic, which worked out great for me because of my own tendency to be hyperactive. We would hang out together all the time. We had similar goals in the field of medicine. We were highly compatible and fell in love eventually. He was from a conventional Indian family that would never allow an out-of-caste marriage. Marriage was such a far-off idea back in college, but we dated anyway. That may have been the biggest mistake I made.

As the years passed, we worked harder to be with each other despite our gruelling training and postgraduate schedules. I was naive and sure of myself back then. When all our capacity for persuasion and our efforts to get our dreams of a lifelong partnership to materialize failed, we decided to part ways to lead more convenient lives. I was heartbroken.

For the first time in my life I felt I had failed utterly at something. For the first time I couldn't see something to the end. People say failure pushes them. However, failure doesn't push me the same way. It took me a long time to heal from this setback.

Did I lose hope? Yes, absolutely. I called my friends, ranted and cried. Sometimes I even questioned my career choice. Did I have to pick such a taxing field? Why didn't I choose an easier path? But, in a strange way, it was my work that kept my head above water. I threw myself into work, offering to take on additional shifts for seniors who were preparing for their exams. I was exhausted to the bone, but it helped me navigate my way through the difficult times. If I hadn't had anything to do, I would have gone crazy.

A year into this emotional turmoil, my life turned around. I found a man who was willing to manage our home and his work at a start-up as well. Our meeting was arranged by our families. I didn't want to hide anything from him before making a commitment. I told him that making money was probably never going to be a problem for me as a neurosurgeon, but I couldn't focus on family and I wouldn't have any time to manage our home. I told him that my work hours were going to be erratic. I wasn't going to promise him anything I couldn't deliver. My work meant everything to me, and I was not willing to let my career, which I'd staked everything on, go. He understood.

Neurosurgery is a conflicting domain. Our success stories are as many as our failures. It is not for the fainthearted. A tiny mistake during brain surgery can leave a patient bedridden for life. You may have saved a patient from dying, but now he may never move. In such a situation, should I, as a doctor, be happy or devastated with the outcome? Families can be broken by neurosurgery. How do I deal with them? These are some of the questions we neurosurgeons grapple with every day at work.

One of the bosses I worked with in residency was terribly smart and was extraordinary at what he did. He was one of the most respected neurosurgeons in India. There was no room for error when you worked with him. He was moody and had a short temper. But it was only natural for him to expect everyone around him to work as hard as he did and be as good at their jobs. I had access to exceptional teachers like him.

Sometimes I ask myself, why have I brought this pain on myself? I could do anything else I set my mind to. In times of self-doubt I remind myself how much I love the brain. When I look at the brain, I don't want to do anything else or be anywhere else. When I am in surgery, I know that I have a person's life in my hands. It's a strange and morbid kind of high that is inexplicable. If I do anything wrong the patient's life can be destroyed. I have to be careful, immensely responsible and highly alert. In a way, the patient's future fully rests in my hands as I begin to operate. As doctors, we don't always have complete control over the outcomes, but the fact that I am contributing to this science every day is good enough for me to keep going. My love for the brain stops me from giving up.

The other reason I persevere is an emotional one. During my postgraduate days, I met a patient with a diabetic foot – he had a wound that just wouldn't heal. He and his wife came from Andhra Pradesh, and none of the doctors in Chandigarh spoke Telugu. Dressing a dirty, infected ulcer is the lowest-rung job in any hospital. I took an interest in them and tried to help them every day. They had absolutely no money. The patient's wife would find work in the fields nearby and bring back a minuscule amount of money to see them through. Often, I would pay for their meals. One day the wife came up to me with a bag of peanuts that she had collected from the farm where she worked. 'Amma,' she said, teary-eyed, 'please take this humble gift from me for taking care of us like our daughter.' I can never forget that moment.

I have seen my father struggle through cancer and I have seen my family brave a financial crisis after his death. I realized early on that health is the only thing that matters in the end. When people don't have money to spend on their health, it's the worst thing that could happen to them. I was driven to become a surgeon because that was my father's last wish, but the reason I continue to be one is that this job gives me opportunities to help people like my father with my own hands.

3

CEO and Fitness Coach: Nilparna Sen

Women make up less than 10 per cent of gym instructors in India[10]

From the very beginning I hated rules. Rules, to me, were meant to be broken. And because of this I wasn't an easy child to deal with.

The earliest childhood memory I have is of being alone at home. My parents had moved from Kolkata to Surat when I was two years old. They had moved in pursuit of better-paying jobs. My mother was an English teacher and my father a financial consultant. Our family had enough money to get by, but never for any luxuries; I had to think twice before I bought a second piece of candy. We lived in a one-bedroom apartment in a middle-class neighbourhood. Nothing about that apartment was striking or fancy. I don't have siblings, and since both my parents were working, my childhood was quite isolated. I found solace in books and music very early on. My solitary upbringing instilled in me a profound sense of loneliness.

I was a misfit in Surat. I grew up into a dour teen, rebellion burning in my belly. I made it my mission to follow no rules and to do whatever I pleased. My mother never bothered me about my studies. I was always an above-average student who did reasonably well at school. But my mother was controlling and demanding about everything else. Her instructions to me were a continuous series of things I shouldn't do:

Don't wear this. Don't hang out with so-and-so. Don't visit friends. Don't do this. Don't do that.

When I was in class nine my mother enrolled me in tuition classes. This was the first time I was able to spend time outside of school and home. The feeling was one of pure freedom. I often bunked tuitions, spending my free time with a guy friend of mine and learning how to ride a bike. The same boy also taught me a terrible new trick – how to smoke – and soon enough I was addicted to smoking.

As adolescence took hold of me, a host of other insecurities and issues too did. I began to feel I wasn't pretty enough. I was an average-looking kid. My body type was also not conventionally feminine. I was stout, had broad shoulders and a square jawline. That my mother was very beautiful made things worse. Whenever we attended a social function together people would often remark, 'Your mother is so beautiful. You look like your father.' That comment stayed with me through my childhood. So I began seeking attention from boys, and found it. I chose to do anything that got me the attention I craved. I once walked up to the most notorious guy in school and kissed him in front of everyone! I wanted to be known as the 'bold' girl. I would tell my pretty girlfriends, 'I've smoked. I've kissed a guy. I've gone to a nightclub. What have you done? You're just pretty.' Being young and naive, I didn't fully understand the repercussions of my choices. Surat was a conservative place, and the things I did ensured that I was the talk of the town. I enjoyed all the attention I got, both good and bad. I was the kid with issues, and I rebelled against everything.

To make matters worse, my parents went through a nasty divorce, which left me very bitter. In a small town like Surat, divorce is a big taboo, and it wasn't long before everyone was talking about my parents. Their divorce broke me. Our entire social circle crumbled after that. Prior to the divorce, my father had a vibrant social life. Now, suddenly, he stopped getting invited to parties and other social gatherings. Humans are social creatures. Being ostracized from society can make life extremely hard for them. The loneliness got to my father. Often, I was his only ray of hope. He would tell me how lonely he felt, breaking down as he spoke. It was heartbreaking to see him like that. Gradually, I distanced myself from him because I hated seeing him so defeated. As a result, my teenage years were one giant, hot mess. I was angry with my parents and I began to drift away from them as a coping mechanism.

The defining characteristics of my childhood were bitterness and bad habits, and it's safe to say that I was miserable. I didn't have role models to urge me to take up a challenge; nor did I have any meaningful benchmarks. No one had ever pushed me out of my comfort zone. I was a bright kid, but not necessarily a hard-working one.

The only reality check I received was when my mother and I visited my grandparents in Kolkata during the summer holidays. My cousins who grew up abroad would also visit Kolkata around the same time. I was fascinated by the way they dressed, the way they spoke and all the things they did. I couldn't connect with them because we didn't share the same context. Also, I felt very inferior to them because it was apparent that I was not polished enough for their company. As a result, all through my childhood, I had a nagging sense of inferiority, which was exacerbated by my mother's unreasonable restrictions and then doubled by my parents' divorce.

The only thing I was sure about was that I needed to get out of Surat, and that could only happen if I went away to college for my undergraduate studies. Many middle-class Indians are mindlessly pushed to pursue IIT-JEE (Joint Entrance Exam) coaching during high school. All my classmates enrolled in JEE coaching, so I did too. However, I found the classes extremely difficult and boring. I would rather have used the extra time to pursue my immediate pleasures. So, in class eleven, I enrolled in commerce instead. I got my shit together for a little while prior to the class twelve board exams because what I wanted most was to leave Surat and, to do that, I knew my grades had to be good. When I finally got admission into a college in Mumbai for media studies, I jumped with joy. And that was that. I packed my bags and, without a second thought, left home in 2011.

I never thought I would fit in in Mumbai. I feared I

would be labelled as a small-town girl, branded as a good-for-nothing or, even worse, that I would be lonely once again. But a big city can work like magic for a small-town misfit, and it wasn't long before I had made some friends.

Around the same time, my father had also found a job in Mumbai. He wanted to stay close to me. He was lonely after his divorce and thought he could take care of me if he stayed in Mumbai.

I should have made better use of being in a metropolis, because there are endless opportunities for those who are looking for them. I could've done something productive and meaningful with my time, but I didn't. My self-destructive nature kicked in, and I spiralled further down the road to ruin. Drugs, clubbing, too many boyfriends and unhealthy relationships – that was my life in a nutshell. My daily routine went something like this – go to bed at 4 a.m., wake up at 4 p.m., dress up, put on make-up, club-hop, drink, smoke, dance, get back to the hostel exhausted, sleep, rinse self and repeat the sequence the next day. My life during the first and second years of college was devoid of purpose. I am ashamed of that version of me now.

In my final year of college in 2014, I was jolted out of my life of fantasy. What was I going to do after graduation? I didn't have good grades; nor had I done anything productive at college that I could put down on my CV. Nobody was going to give me a job. Advertising was an option I could pursue, but I didn't know anything about it and I wasn't convinced I had the aptitude for it.

After much deliberation, I decided to take a year off after graduation, move back to Surat and prepare for the CAT (Common Admission Test) examination in the hope of pursuing an MBA.

I was not ambitious about anything during this phase. I just wanted a decent job that paid me enough so I could continue to enjoy the hedonistic pleasures of life. Nothing about my thought process or life choices was exceptional. I was a mediocre kid. All I wanted to do was to dress up and go clubbing, but I needed money to do that. It was necessary for me to get a job to keep up the lifestyle I desired. During this break I had lots of time on my hands. Little did I know that I was going to make a decision that would inadvertently change my life forever.

The reason I first joined a gym was superficial. I wanted to look better so more boys would be attracted to me. As the first month went by I was stunned by my progress – I could see visible changes in my body. I began to love looking at myself in the mirror, amazed by the changes. The concept of transformation was new to me. I had never understood the symbiotic relationship between effort and results because I had never worked hard enough at anything. But for the first time in my life I now tasted the high of improvement and results. Suddenly, I made the connection: if I ran three kilometres on a treadmill today, I could push that number higher if I just put in a little more effort. It was such a simple light bulb that went off in my head! It may sound funny to you, but it was the first time that I realized the value of hard work. Gradually, I started becoming addicted to this new high.

Just like most people who begin to gym, I started with cardio and began to experience fat loss in the first few months. When I saw the results, I began to crave other goals. Perhaps I could tone my entire body? My thighs and arms, specifically? I conducted extensive research online and found that weight training was the surest way to a toned body. Unlike the popular perception, weightlifting doesn't bulk women up. In fact, it makes us lean and results in much faster fat loss than any other form of cardio. I consulted the trainer at the local Talwalkars gym, and he gave me a training regimen to follow.

Soon my arms started getting stronger and my body tighter. I vividly remember feeling my biceps for the first time. I looked at myself in the mirror and said to myself, 'You have created this all on your own!'

Surprisingly, as I became result and goal oriented at the gym, that mindset slowly started percolating into every other area of my life. I quit drinking and smoking. I rectified my sleeping pattern. My room used to be a mess before; now I kept it clean. Gradually, the fog in my life began to clear too. Going to the gym became addictive. Never before had I experienced the fruits of hard work and discipline.

The reason I started going to the gym was a shallow and selfish one, but oddly enough it turned out to be my biggest spiritual transformation. I was experiencing philosophical growth for the first time. And, to be honest, the reason I took a break after graduation to prepare for CAT was that I was lazy and shying away from real life. It was just a silly excuse for a break. I never once thought it would turn out to be the most profound break of my life! Up until that time, I had only experienced the pleasures of drugs, sex and partying, but after my stint at the gym I began experiencing the pleasures of improvement, discipline and the glory of health and fitness.

I signed up for a fitness certification course in Mumbai. On weekdays I would study for CAT, and then every weekend I would take the train to Mumbai to attend the fitness classes. My entire day was spent researching nutrition and body transformation. I would endlessly watch YouTube videos and train by myself. Midway through the fitness course in Mumbai I had another revelation. I realized that the fitness industry in India was still in its nascent stage and that the opportunities it offered were limitless. There was a huge knowledge gap in the industry too. It was very difficult to find a good coach who could also communicate well with customers. In many cases, the coaches were not aware of the latest health and fitness trends. As my interest in the fitness sector deepened, I started building connections in the industry and began to nurture them. No matter how archaic the fitness industry in Surat was, it had still changed my fucking life! I wanted to give back to this industry by being part of it, but I wasn't 100 per cent sure about the choice.

A month before my CAT exam, I got a call from

revered celebrity fitness guru Kaizzad Capadia, founder of the K11 Fitness Academy. He had seen my workout and fitness posts on Instagram and decided to reach out to me. Kaizzad told me about the various trends in the fitness world and what was lacking in India. He encouraged me to pursue fitness as a full-time career. The hour-long conversation with him left me overwhelmed and on top of the world. It made me take a leap of faith. It was just the nudge I had needed to plunge right in.

As my conviction deepened I decided to have the difficult conversation with my father. That I wanted to be a fitness trainer would be unacceptable. I came from a Bengali family of highly educated people. Most of my uncles and aunts are PhDs. Finally, I told him that he needed to trust my decision, that I had enough marks to get into a decent MBA programme, but what I really wanted was to pursue fitness because I had a deep calling for the industry. I was sure he wouldn't understand my choice and that he would say no. And so I was shocked when he said, 'If you make this choice then become the very best at it.' After that day my relationship with my father changed for the better. We grew closer and gradually began to derive strength from our relationship.

I had a choice to make at this point. I could either move back to Mumbai to work with Kaizzad, which would have been a dream come true, or stay back in Surat and join a local gym. It was a hard decision to make, but in the end, I chose Surat. The place I'd once been desperate to get away from was where I was going to start my career! Ironic, isn't it? I decided I would own the fitness scene in Surat, improving its standards and infusing fresh blood into it. I wanted to be part of a change that I could envision, and lead on my own. In Mumbai, I would be one among hundreds of trainers. In Surat I had the possibility of leading from the front. Mumbai was a no-brainer. But I chose the difficult path instead.

During that time, I came to learn that a leading businessman was opening a massive gym facility, called KG Fitness, in Surat. It was equipped with state-of-the-art world-class facilities. I immediately joined as a trainer.

Going to the gym had been a big high, but I didn't realize how exhilarating coaching would be. Helping other people with their goals is a different experience altogether. One's scope for growth as a trainer is limitless. You have to deal with different body types and psychological profiles because every client is a unique challenge. The learning process is endless. To be a good trainer you must keep learning and unlearning every single day.

Early in my career, I was keen to train women because physical strength as a value is never associated with us. Society had laid down the rules for this a long time ago, and I, the rule-breaker, wanted to change things. I wanted to help women get stronger. I was lucky with my initial set of clients. I could sense that my female clients were attracted to my body type. They'd never seen a lean, muscular and toned woman with strong shoulders, firm glutes and flat abs. They wanted to look like me.

The crème de la crème of Surat began to train with me,

and they wanted to show off their progress in their social circles, which was a good thing for me. I leveraged that aspect and worked hard on them. As their bodies began to transform, my popularity in Surat grew. My clients eventually let go of the idea of training to be skinny; they began training to be strong. In the process, I began to fall in love with my home town. I was grateful for the opportunity Surat had given me, and now I was convinced that my role was to shape Surat's fitness scene.

I never trained people for money. I trained them because I loved every minute of it. But that's life, isn't it? Once you put in the hard work and you are true to what you do, financial rewards will inevitably follow.

I had joined a brand-new facility, and so it was only natural for me to be curious about every aspect of the business. I wanted to understand how every machine worked. I wanted to understand how sales, accounts and marketing worked. I'd train clients six hours a day, and then spend the rest of my time as a sales representative. I loved being a sales rep because it helped me understand customer profiles – What did people want? What were their aspirations? Two years later, the management saw my loyalty and commitment, and promoted me to manager.

I never thought I was ready to be a manager because I didn't know a thing about management. I learned that one is never fully ready for anything; the best strategy is always to jump into things and figure them out along the way. My new role was challenging initially, but I soon learned the ropes of the job. In 2017, I was promoted to CEO! Who would have thought my journey would turn out like this? From a mediocre alcoholic and wastrel to CEO of Surat's largest gym!

At twenty-five, I have to run an organization of 100 people, and where 90 per cent of the staff are older than me. It is highly challenging. I've been working hard ever since I joined the fitness industry, but now I must exhaust every skill I have and learn new ones to truly succeed. Being a trainer is like being an artist who shapes people, but being a CEO comes with its own conflicts. As a CEO, I have to prioritize and often many of these priorities are in conflict with each other. Now I have to worry about the company's financial health, think about cost-cutting and growing profits on the balance sheet while also keeping the customer's best interests in mind.

My dream is to open multiple branches of KG Fitness worldwide and also improve the fitness industry in India. Less than 1 per cent of Indians subscribe to a gym membership. I want that number to go up to 50 per cent. I have developed the mindset of an achiever. I am learning to handle one task at a time and not get overwhelmed. I have learned the importance of hard work, but now I'm also learning to understand my own psyche and how to manage it. When I was younger, my father worried constantly about how I didn't care enough about my career. Now he worries about how obsessed I have become with it! And I love the fact that I've surprised him.

I would be lying if I said I never went back to drinking

and drugs along my journey. But on the days I did, guilt would not let me sleep at night. Now I know better. I am way too obsessed with bodybuilding and the fitness industry to allow distractions to come in my way.

Elle magazine featured me in an article in 2017, placing me alongside many celebrities. But I don't let external validation distract me from my larger goal. I don't coach people to become a celebrity. I coach because I want to help people get fit and stay healthy.

Today, when young people ask me for advice, I know what to say. Put in the work, get better at something, experience the pleasure of improvement, transformation and mastery, and your life will never be the same again. If it worked for me, it's got to work for you too!

4

Artist: Shilo Shiv Suleman

Out of the fifty highest-earning Indian artists, eight are women[11]

I am Shilo Shiv Suleman, daughter of Nilofer Suleman. My mother is not only the source of my life, but also my biggest source of inspiration and strength. We are both artists, and when we first started off in the art world nobody knew anything about us.

My friends called me Padmapada (the one with lotus feet) when I was growing up. My mother's name, Nilofer, means the 'blue lotus'. Just like lotuses that blossom in the murkiest of waters, my mother and I braved many difficulties that life threw at us and we thrived. The symbol of the lotus appears frequently in my paintings and installations. You can spot it everywhere in my art, and now you know why.

My mother grew up in Indore. Her father was a progressive man who was a strong advocate of education for girls. He encouraged all his daughters to pursue literature and to read voraciously. My mother went on a road trip to many places in India with her best friend before getting married, which was practically unheard of in the 1980s. She was always ahead of her time. She, a Muslim, married a Hindu. And because of my eclectic upbringing I consider myself half Muslim, half Hindu. My friends say I can't be a half Muslim, that one is either a Muslim or not. I tell them I am a full Muslim and a full Hindu then.

I was born in Singapore in 1989. My earliest childhood memories are of having my mother by my bedside whenever I woke up. She always knew when I would be up, and no matter what time I opened my eyes, she was there, like a rock. Even as a child I knew that my mother would be around to help me cross any hurdles that were going to come my way. This knowledge gave me tremendous strength and confidence.

When I was five we moved back to India because my parents separated. My mother found herself in Bengaluru as a single parent, with no financial means.

Thankfully, my mother had had a good education. She had studied psychology and cartography. In Singapore, she used to make beautiful maps. She used her skill and started teaching art classes at schools in Bengaluru. In her free time, she painted to support our family. In a way, art also helped her heal from a marriage that didn't work out. People often think art is a means of escape, but that could not be further from the truth. Art has the unparalleled ability to capture and draw you into the present moment. Art has the power to give you brutal clarity.

My mother was single-mindedly driven to give me and my brother, Shaan, the best life she could possibly afford. She gave classes at school during the day, conducted painting classes for children at home in the evenings, and then would work on her own paintings through the night. I don't know when she slept!

It was my mother's goal to do whatever it took to enrol Shaan and me into a good school. She finally enrolled us at The Valley School – an alternative school located in the middle of a lush forest on the outskirts of Bengaluru. The school was based on the teachings of the philosopher Jiddu Krishnamurti. It helped that my mother taught art at the same school.

For as long as I can remember, I bunked all maths and physics classes, and my teachers often complained about this to my mother. But instead of hauling me up for my naughtiness, my mother would stand up for me, arguing that my interest lay in art, and that perhaps maths and the sciences were not interesting enough to capture my attention. The teachers would be shocked by my mother's reaction. Many parents panic at the first complaint they receive from teachers, without fully understanding their child's inclinations. My mother fiercely protected my passion for the arts and gave me the platform to pursue my interests. It's important for parents to recognize their children's interests, because when children are pushed to do what they love they will naturally flourish.

When I was twelve, I began helping my mother with her art classes, and I spent all my free time painting. My mother took note of my dedication, and so she never once forced me to do anything else. Instead, she encouraged me to invest time in honing my craft. As a result, I spent many hours painting, making illustrations and getting better at my craft. I never waited for inspiration to start work. I just painted every day without judging what I was making. I would encourage any aspiring artist to be prolific.

My other favourite activity at school was running around and exploring the forest. It's wonderful for children to have access to expansive, vast spaces; it brings in them a sense of calm and confidence. My best friend, Gayathri, and I spent hours exploring the terrain, climbing trees and running after animals. She and I practically grew up together. She is a photographer now, and we continue to collaborate on many projects.

Growing up, I was the 'artist' type who didn't do well at 'real' subjects, such as maths and the sciences. According to my teachers at school, I was not fit for the actual world. There was no doubt or debate about the fact that I would go to art college after school. I enrolled in a four-year design course at Srishti Institute of Art and Design in Bengaluru. It was at Srishti that I flourished and was always at the top of my class. This is where I truly shone and, for the first time, belonged. I would work on several art projects day and night, and my teachers adored me for my dedication.

When I turned sixteen, inspired by the stories of my mother's travels, I too set off on my first-ever solo trip across the country. This was not an expensive holiday. We didn't have much money at the time. I took Rs 1000, bought myself a seat on the cheapest bus available, and headed out. The experience was life-changing. I was pushed out of my comfort zone. I met new people and learnt how to fend for myself. After that first trip I was hooked. I loved travelling by train in the third-class compartment and sharing food and beedis with strangers. Travel was my way of discovering myself, seeking independence and developing a point of view about the world. Travel can be a wonderful teacher because it nullifies fear. In India, we are made to think that travelling alone is dangerous, especially for girls, but when you finally do go out on your own you'll be surprised by the kindness of people. We need to let go of the fear that holds us back. I am not saying that bad things won't happen. They will. But you can't let that fear paralyse you into inaction. I want us to live as if the best things will happen to us.

I am a thorough Internet kid. Blogging was a natural progression for me. I used it as a platform to showcase my illustrations of my travels. When I was seventeen, I was commissioned to do a book of illustrations; hence I am fully aware of the value the Internet brought to my life.

There is a deep need to constantly sell in the world today. I am an artist who creates for the sake of creating and I have tremendous respect for others who do the same. Think about it – do flowers need to explain why they are beautiful? We need to make space for more non-verbal experiences. Having said that, artists, as a community, do need to be able to communicate their work to the world.

At the end of the day, art is a form of communication, and some of the most successful artists that ever lived have all been loud advocates of their art. They don't shy away from putting their art out there for the world to scrutinize. In the beginning, my mother was a struggling artist in every sense of the word, but she never shied away from engaging with the world. She had to. She had two children to support and she was determined to give them a beautiful life. I take a similar approach. I don't look at money as a dirty thing. I understand its value. Many artists in India don't promote their own art; they think it goes against the idea of being an 'artist'. But art will not reach its audiences on its own. I constantly share my art with the world. If you are keen to be in the creative world you should leverage the existing social media platforms to showcase your work and receive feedback. A world of opportunities will open up to you.

My career got a big boost when I was twenty-one. K.K. Raghava, now my friend and mentor, had exhibited his works at the same galleries as my mother. He was looking up my mother online when he accidentally found my blog. I was nineteen when he came over to our house. He went through all my illustrations and was pleased with my work. Since that day Raghava has had a huge impact on me. A couple of years later, Raghava called me to tell me he was bringing Lakshmi Pratury over to meet me. Lakshmi is an exceptionally well-connected person; she brought the TED conference to India in 2009, which was hosted in Mysore. She is always on the lookout for undiscovered, budding young talent that she can nurture and showcase to the world. Lakshmi loved my work, gave me an opportunity to speak at TED and selected me as an INK Fellow. That one meeting with Lakshmi changed my life.

Immediately after my TED talk, my followership on social media exploded. My email was flooded with messages from strangers. But even though the TED talk was a success, I never once felt as if I had made it or that my job was done. I knew that this was all part of a long journey. I remember going through the YouTube comments on my TED video. While there were many positive comments, there were also innumerable trolls. There were a few comments that really upset me. I sought the counsel of a few people who were used to being in the public eye on how to deal with online bashing. What they told me surprised and, oddly, comforted me. I learnt that everyone who is a public figure experiences some amount of trolling. I was not alone.

In 2012, I was in Delhi to attend a friend's wedding when news of the brutal Delhi gang rape broke. That evening, people took to the streets of Delhi to protest. When I heard the news, I was so disturbed that I immediately went to join the protests. While the energy of the protests was truly incredible, there was so much fearmongering in the media around that time. It felt counterproductive to achieving the change we were seeking in society. I was constantly bombarded with messages such as, 'Don't go out at night, you'll get raped.' 'Don't attract too much attention, you'll get raped.' 'Don't take a bus, don't walk alone, and don't walk with a single man.' I thought to myself that we don't need any more fear perpetuated in our society. If anything, we need women reclaiming public spaces fearlessly. Maybe then the rapes will stop?

In response to the Delhi gang rape, I made and shared a poster of a woman with her hands crossed over her body on my Facebook page. The poster read, 'I never ask for it. Fearless.' Immediately, many women from across the world began to respond to my poster with personal stories about their relationship with fear and love. The submissions came from all kinds of women who had reported violence, climbed mountains, travelled alone, left abusive relationships, started companies, and quit their jobs to pursue something they loved. These women were seemingly ordinary, but did radical things. I wanted to take the power of these online conversations on to the streets through art.

Around the same time, I was on a road trip to the Kumbh Mela with my boyfriend at the time at the back of a motorcycle. I was immersed in the world's largest spiritual gathering asking myself, 'Why do we worship women in our temples but rape them at our homes and on our streets?' During this trip, a sadhu in Uttar Pradesh said to me, 'If you want to treat yourself like a goddess, do it yourself. Why do you want somebody else to do it?' As a response to that comment, I made a huge painting of Goddess Durga with a cat and a little girl looking up at her. The painting says, 'What we worship, we shall become.' That painting still adorns a wall near the banks of the Ganga. This was one of the first few paintings I had done on the streets after the Delhi gang rape to set a stage for reclaiming space for women in our society.

Since then, I began using art to nurture fearlessness in women. Eventually, I started an organization called The Fearless Collective, where we use art as a tool to teach communities to be braver. We offer art-based workshops and community-led public art projects to replace fear with love in public spaces.

Until this moment, art to me was a personal exploration of wonder, technology and beauty. But now, I felt that I needed to use my art to heal the trauma in the world. Engaging in art and participating in its creation has the potential to change people. My mother and I are examples of the power of art.

I poured most of the money I made from my personal commissioned art projects into The Fearless Collective projects. For almost five years I didn't draw a salary for the work I did there. I work day and night. I take on commissioned projects so that I can feed that capital into Fearless projects. While my personal artwork is bought by rich people for their homes and offices, my mural and art installation projects via The Fearless Collective enable me to take art to the most excluded communities.

My work through The Fearless Collective has taken me to places I have never been to before. I began this journey locally in India, but grew in size eventually to take on projects from the world over. We worked with diverse communities such as the daughters of sex workers in Delhi, Syrian and Armenian refugees in Beirut, women who live in Dharavi, the Tupinamba people of Bahia, Brazil, and kids from Kathmandu, Nepal.

I painted a 100-foot mural of a sex worker and her daughter in Lodhi Colony, Delhi. Sex workers and their daughters have been rejected by society. I included a diverse set of people in this project – including some sex workers themselves, their daughters, regular housewives from the colony, policemen and local sweepers – to paint the mural alongside me.

I have done several street art projects in slums across Pakistan. We raised a grant from the United States Institute for Peace to do art-based workshops and public art projects in Pakistan.

In Johannesburg, South Africa, I did a huge street art project in collaboration with a community of local women. The painting says, 'I wear my body without shame.'

My friends ask me if I don't feel afraid to visit so many unknown places. 'Does your mother worry? What if something happens?' The answer is yes; I was scared in the beginning. Immediately after I started The Fearless Collective, I went on a road trip with a friend to Uttar Pradesh. Groups of men would unflinchingly stare at me wherever we stopped. I felt myself physically shrinking each time this happened. I would lower my gaze and lose my confidence in these circumstances. It was like an instinctive reaction. It was baffling. There I was, founder of The Fearless Collective, terrified! My own behaviour made me experience feelings of deep unrest. If my goal was to use art to eradicate violence, how could I be so scared myself?

When I spoke to a friend about what I was going through, she said, 'The world reflects your fears and your emotions. Show strength and maybe you'll see strength reflected,' she told me. It made sense to me as I brooded over her advice.

The next day, I was on the road again. When a group of men started staring at me, I didn't lower my gaze. I looked at them unapologetically in the eye, and asked, '*Kya hua?*' That broke the ice, and one of them asked me: '*Kahan ja rahe ho?*' That moment changed my life. Since then, I replace fear with love as my everyday practice And that's the point of my art – to be fearless and to weave fearlessness and love into the fabric of communities.

The Fearless Collective has been a massive learning experience. The group has grown from a one-woman outfit to six full-time people and thousands of volunteers the world over. We are currently working on an art campaign to explore how gender and environment are interconnected. I drew my first salary from The Fearless Collective five years after I started it, and as an entrepreneur and an artist, it's a great milestone for me to have gotten to this stage. Art gives me the opportunity to heal and to make the world a better place. Art saved both my mother's life and mine, and it's a privilege to be able to share that joy with others.

My travel schedule is crazy. I work every waking moment of my life. 'How do you do it?' 'Don't you get tired?' 'What keeps you going?' These are the questions I'm always asked.

I have attempted to cultivate an abundance mindset when it comes to money and time. I want to feel like I always have enough. The idea of having enough is all in your mind. When I was a teenager, I thought Rs 1000 was enough for a week-long trip. It often wasn't, but I wasn't stressed about it. I am never frantic about getting to the airport in time; even if I'm running late I don't panic. I will calmly shower, put on my make-up and get an auto or cab. And, let me tell you, I've never missed a flight till date. I've realized that worrying does not get you anywhere. I want to operate from a position of fearlessness in how I manage my money, time, investments, relationships and projects. It's a way of life for me. My manager jokes about my approach to time; she says I behave as if I have all the time in the world. I laugh it off and call it an abundance mindset.

As an artist, I have to keep feeding my soul. For me, inspiration comes through reading. I read poetry, and I love mythology and non-fiction. I am fond of old-school Tamil Sangam poetry, and some of it is very erotic and luscious. I always carry a collection of Sufi poems with me no matter where I go, and I read a bunch of them every day.

I believe that when you do something it has to be true at three levels: it has to be true to every atom in your body, true to everyone around you and true to every star and every galaxy in the universe.

5

Physics Professor: Prerna Sharma

Prerna is the first female physics professor hired by IISc in twenty-seven years[12]

'You need to study hard to succeed,' my father would tell my brother and me all the time. 'Business is for losers. It breaks families. Business is a dirty business.' He ingrained this sentiment in us early on. My father was not a religious person, but we had our own kind of religion at home. 'You can't drink or smoke, and you have to be sincere students.' That was my father's religion.

    My father grew up in Daryaganj, Delhi. His mother was a housewife and his father a clerk in the local court. They had ten children, and my father was the eighth. With one breadwinner and ten children it was very hard for the family to make ends meet. My father delivered water cans after school to support the family. He had a difficult upbringing, as his family was in a shambles financially. Often, they didn't have enough money to pay their electricity bill. My father would study at his neighbours' houses or under street lamps. Except for my father and a couple of his siblings who focused on education, none of the other children were able to break out of the poverty cycle. The siblings who didn't focus on education started their own small businesses, all of which failed miserably. Those experiences clouded my father's judgement about business.

With hard work and dedication, my father excelled at his studies. He got a seat at St Stephen's College, Delhi University, to study physics. My grandparents were worried about his choice. 'Why are you turning down engineering to study pure sciences at a college that rich people send their children to? How will you fit in?' But by then my father had made up his mind. He knew that education at a reputed college was going to be his only recourse. My father came out of extreme poverty through sheer determination and resilience.

My father worked in the customs department. When I was very young, we moved from Delhi to Jaipur. I went to a Kendriya Vidyalaya. Naturally, as my father's child, I was the 'padhaku' type, an obedient and duty-bound kid. To be honest, I couldn't excel at anything except academics.

I wasn't an athletic kid. Once, the entire class had to participate in a race and there was no way I could back out. That evening I came home super happy. My mother asked me if I had won something, and I told her that for the first time I hadn't fallen flat on my face on the track! Usually I never even bothered to complete these races.

I didn't enjoy any activity that involved an audience either. The first time I had to perform on stage, I froze. I promised myself then that I wouldn't ever step on to a stage again. I was painfully shy. I never had more than two or three friends at school. Even when I was young, I would invest well in the relationships I did have, and having any more friends was exhausting. I never understood the popular kids who hung out with huge crowds.

My teachers were my gods, and I worshipped them for their knowledge. I knew that only the obedient class-toppers could get a teacher's attention and affection, and so I spent all my primary school years seeking that kind of validation. I was a true nerd!

When I was in class five, my parents decided to move back to Delhi because they thought it would be better for our studies. My father soon got himself transferred. Delhi took a physical toll on me. In Jaipur, I used to walk to school. In Delhi, the auto ride to school was on extremely congested and polluted roads. I was exhausted all the time. The Delhi experience, in terms of schooling, was also harsh on me. In Jaipur, everyone was super quiet and polite, but in this new city my classmates treated me like a small-town girl. Very soon I learned that I would have to fend for myself to survive.

Maths and the sciences were my thing; I excelled at them. When it comes to subjects such as English, the social sciences and civics, students are graded subjectively. But with maths and the sciences, there can only be one right answer, and I loved that surety about them. I loved chemistry more than physics, and this irked my father, who believed that a strong physics education prepared you for anything in the world.

When I got to class eleven, physics got especially harder. I sucked at it, but I stuck to it like a dog to a bone. I was not a rebellious child, and I was always agreeing to most things my parents asked me to do. My father didn't want me majoring in chemistry, so I had to figure out a way to excel at physics. I was a fighter, and resilience had been ingrained in me. I read my textbooks line by line repeatedly, slowly trying to make sense of the formulae and decipher the theories. In class twelve I had a wonderful teacher, and physics eventually became fun. I will always be grateful to that teacher.

I decided I would pursue the pure sciences as a career option. I wanted to be an academician. Many people warned me that the sciences become extremely difficult as you go forward. The refrain I heard from everyone was, 'Why don't you become an engineer?' But by then my heart was set on the pure sciences.

My father had a slightly different take on it. 'You can pursue science, but only if you get admission into the best college in India for pure sciences,' he told me. And St Stephen's was the college he had in mind. I accepted his challenge. My father always dreamed of one of his kids getting into St Stephen's and continuing the family legacy. My father is eternally grateful to his alma mater for giving him the edge over other candidates when it came to job opportunities. Since my brother had taken up hotel management, I had to be the one to make my father's dream a reality. I didn't disappoint him. He was the happiest man on earth when I got into St Stephen's.

I understood the value of the English language only after I joined St Stephen's. College was a melting pot of people from all over India, and being fluent in English meant you could communicate with everyone. The humanities students were a hip bunch. The science students were modest and nerdy. As a result, the science students found it difficult to make friends with the humanities bunch. Today, I know from experience that both sides would have benefited a lot from interacting with each other.

I am the kind of girl who likes to sit in a corner and observe people. Often, people mistake my shyness for pride or arrogance. Thankfully, I've never cared about what people think of me. But my lack of social skills did prove a challenge when I got into St Stephen's. I was a quiet student, always hesitating to ask questions. In fact, I rarely opened my mouth in class, and so no one noticed me. The students who were loud and expressive were considered intelligent by the teachers. I was very intimidated by these students. I was so afraid to ask the teachers for help in public that I would go to their offices after class to clarify my doubts. I was shy in social situations too. At eighteen, at my cousin's wedding, I couldn't even ask the guy at the counter to serve me more food. I had to ask my mother to do it for me!

I struggled through my first semester at St Stephen's. But I'm tenacious, and I don't give up at the first sight of trouble. I go back to things I don't understand and work at them till I do. A couple of semesters later people started noticing that I was silently topping the class. No student or teacher saw that coming.

Many people assume that passion strikes us suddenly, like lightning. They wait all their lives for that moment, hoping that things will automatically get easier. This is far from the truth. Nobody is good at anything when they are just starting out. People get better and more skilled with time, practice, consistency and commitment to their craft. We also tend to enjoy what we become good at. Honing your skill is the surest way to enjoy doing something and building your confidence, and it doesn't work the other way around.

My undergraduate days were only dedicated to academics. I never had a boyfriend, and I did not bunk classes or watch movies either. I spent all my free time studying, attending classes or doing internships during the holidays. I was conscious of the money my parents gave me. Every day my father would give me Rs 20 for the commute to college and back. On some days when he was in a good mood it would be Rs 50. I would spend Rs 10 on the commute and save the remaining money to go to Kamla Nagar and buy used physics books.

I knew I could not waste money that was not mine. I was in class seven when my brother decided to pursue hotel management. I overheard my parents say to each other that they didn't have enough money to pay for my brother's college fees the next semester. They were worried about how they'd find the Rs 40,000 that was his admission fee. My parents had worked hard all their lives to put my brother and me through college, and I was careful about any little extra expenditure. In fact, I felt ashamed of myself when I asked them for money to watch a movie with friends during my final semester at St Stephen's.

By the time I graduated, I absolutely loved physics, but I still wasn't sure if I was capable of making original breakthroughs or adding any real value to the field. Even though I was a gold medallist at St Stephen's, I didn't know if I had it in me to do a PhD. I was always plagued by a lack of confidence. I mulled over my prospects all the time. Did I have the quantitative and analytical skills needed to be a good researcher? I wrote the JAM (Joint Admission Test for MSc) and JEST (Joint Entrance Screening Test) exams for admission to prestigious pure sciences institutions in India for higher studies. Only serious academicians sit for these exams, and only serious academicians grade them. I was ranked fiftieth (out of 4000 students from across the country) in the JAM test, and seventieth in the JEST. This boosted my confidence and helped me make my decision. I went ahead with the PhD. I got admission into the Tata Institute of Fundamental Research (TIFR), one of the premier research institutes of India. I didn't make it to the Indian Institute of Science (IISc) then. Isn't it ironic that I now teach at IISc?

Studying at TIFR was the hardest thing I've ever done. It was a drastic change from my otherwise routine life. First, I had to move to Mumbai, where I had to live in a hostel. For the first time ever, I had to do all my chores myself, including the laundry, cleaning, washing and other jobs, and this added to my already gruelling schedule. I hated the food I was eating. The classes were taxing, and competitive too because ours was a class of only twenty. I had only one other female colleague there. I was homesick all the time. I was amazed at how I'd taken everything for granted back at home, and I felt a new sense of profound gratitude for my parents.

At an integrated physics programme like the one in TIFR, everyone is super smart and deeply passionate about the subject. They wouldn't have made it this far if that weren't the case. During my first semester at TIFR I was at the bottom of the class. And this terrified me. Just the way computer science is the favoured specialization after engineering, theoretical physics was the prize in our field back then. But one needed the grades and the right thesis adviser to complete a PhD. Since my grades weren't good, my hopes of choosing theoretical physics for my thesis work suddenly came crashing down. With very few open positions for theoretical physics, I was 100 per cent sure I was not going to make the cut. So I started to look for research advisers in other areas. The fears and challenges at this stage are slightly different. 'How do I pick the right research problem to work on?' 'Who is a suitable PhD adviser for me?' 'What if I can't complete my thesis?' These questions kept me up most nights.

Dr Shankar Ghosh was a faculty member at TIFR who had become a professor at age thirty – which is almost unheard of in academic circles. Dr Ghosh was a bright young scientist who was popular on campus. Students loved him and looked up to him. I attended some of his lectures and was blown away by his dynamism. At last I had found what I wanted to do. I joined Dr Ghosh's lab, where we did research on soft matter physics.

To be trained by Dr Ghosh was the best thing that ever happened to me. Dr Ghosh was a demanding teacher, someone who kept his students on their toes. He had a sharp mind, was very opinionated and wasn't ever afraid to speak up. He gave his students twenty-four hours to solve a problem and to conduct an experiment. If you failed to do so within the given time, he would solve the problem himself the next day within no time! He was proving a point to us – that there is an answer to all problems. We just had to find out how to crack it. Being in his lab mostly felt like being in a pressure cooker! The classes were intense. I had to work overtime just to be considered even halfway decent! In the beginning, I didn't even know how to set up and calibrate lab equipment. How could Dr Ghosh solve a problem in five minutes when I couldn't do it in twenty-four hours? I would watch him like a hawk as he solved problems, and slowly I began picking up those skills. It took me several months to bring myself up to speed at his lab.

Beneath Dr Ghosh's strong and abrasive personality lies a considerate and compassionate teacher who understands his students' shortcomings, goals and worries. He was highly perceptive of his students' abilities. The problems he gave me to solve were only slightly above my current level of ability, even though I always had to push myself to arrive at the solution. It took us some time to figure out what he was trying to achieve with his students, and once we understood that we were in total awe of him. Dr Ghosh gave his students a sense of purpose every day; he kept us motivated, and as a result physics became joyful. He pushed me very hard, and this meant spending many intense days in the lab to complete an experiment. Nothing less than excellence was expected from me. He prepared me well for the world out there. The value he added to my life is immeasurable. I have known Dr Ghosh for over a decade now, and he is like family to me. At twenty-eight, I became a professor at IISc, and this was possible only because of his training.

When the second semester results were declared, I was stumped. There were only two in our batch who had passed that exam. And I was one of them! I couldn't believe it. Here were the brightest minds of physics in the country under one roof, and 90 per cent of them had failed that exam. And I, who had been at the bottom of my class earlier, had made the cut!

I have always been a climber. It takes me some time to adjust to a new situation and to learn the ropes, but once I do there is no stopping me. My persistence and commitment enabled me to win in the long run. Most people give up at the first sign of trouble, but I don't. I have overcome temporary setbacks all my life. To me, setbacks are just that – temporary. And one needs to work through them. Setbacks are stepping stones to success; if you can hold this mantra close to your heart, know that you'll come out a winner in the long run.

The results gave me a big boost of confidence. Suddenly, I realized that I could take up any theory position I wanted. But by then I was addicted to the lab work with Dr Ghosh. I loved it and I didn't want to leave it for any theoretical physics position. This was a big learning moment for me. I realized that most of us decide what is cool and what is not based on what others think. Often, we do this without any real personal experience to back our conclusions. When I joined TIFR, I too bought into the popular perception that theoretical physics was more distinguished than lab work, and I had been disheartened when I couldn't take it up because of my bad grades. And yet, there I was, with both options finally open to me, but this time around I had found my calling. Life has a funny way of working out. Many students in India fall into this trap and end up stuck in areas of study they don't love. My advice to them would be to keep an open and curious mind and try out new experiences before they make any decisions. When someone tells a student 'this is better than that', I would encourage the student to pause and to challenge those perceptions. People who give blanket advice usually don't know what they are talking about. The decision must come from you, and you alone.

At St Stephen's, a third of my class was female. Once I got into the PhD programme, those numbers dropped significantly. One thing stood out for me, though.

Even if the women constituted only a small fraction of the class, they were all extraordinary. The ten girls at St Stephen's were intelligent and hard-working. In the PhD programme, the one female colleague I had did seminal work in string theory – one of the most intellectually challenging subjects there is in the world. The number of female researchers is very low. But I never felt I didn't have role models. All I had to do was to look at my small set of peers.

Six years later, I had completed my PhD at Dr Ghosh's lab. I wanted to experience what it was like to do research work outside India and asked my parents about it. When they gave me their blessings, Dr Ghosh helped me with a strong recommendation to get a postdoc position in Boston.

Life in Boston was both challenging and harsh. The winters were brutally cold. I had changed my research subject, and everything was unfamiliar to the point where I couldn't even set up my Internet connection. Imagine a scientist struggling to get her Internet working! I was homesick and lonely. I called my parents often; they had never seen me so distraught before. But as I got my bearings, things started to improve. Boston is the quintessential university town. The peer group of researchers is a tight-knit community that is proactive with feedback and encouragement. As a result, my research on biopolymers picked up pace. Plus, Dr Ghosh's training and his emphasis on independent thinking worked wonders for me there. In Boston one must figure things out oneself, and many Indian students struggle with this kind of working style. You may get some direction on the approach, but you won't get any spoon-feeding there. But Dr Ghosh had already trained me to adapt to this new environment.

I was certain of one thing: that I would eventually come back to India to work. I wanted to live close to my parents and teach in my own country. When I came to India during the holidays, I would often visit many research centres and volunteer to give lectures on soft matter physics. I made myself visible in the physics community even during the two years that I was in Boston. The fact that my work had also been published in reputed international publications was a bonus. Even before I had completed my postdoc, I received offers from both IISc and TIFR. IISc was the more lucrative offer, and it allowed me time to continue my research work.

Physics is the crutch I use to overcome my extreme shyness. Even to this day, if you put me in a social situation I am usually uncomfortable. I find it hard to make any conversation. But throw me in a room full of physics scholars, and my fear will fade, even if only momentarily! My shyness is in striking contrast to the number of speeches and public lectures I give for my work. I get my biggest high when I am looking into the microscope. It's thrilling to have a new problem to solve. When I see data that I can't immediately make sense of, I get excited. I know that I'll have to spend some quality time deciphering the data, and I love that feeling. I go to work for that joy.

The discovery of graphene – a remarkable substance used in batteries, touchscreens, computer chips, etc. – took a decade. Scientific research requires patience, perseverance and commitment. There is no instant gratification. Science is a long-haul career. It takes anywhere between five and seven years to finish a PhD, and another two years to complete postdoc work. Unlike engineering, where one can find a job immediately after graduating, a PhD student must wait ten years after college to begin earning a salary. It needs grit and determination to be a scientist.

I was shocked to find out that I was the first female professor hired by the physics department at IISc in twenty-seven years. The revelation was disheartening. Many women do PhDs, but most of them don't become tenured professors. Some of the brightest peers I had through my college years were women, but now I have to struggle to find female peers.

Perhaps one of the reasons most Indian women don't pursue research work is that in this field transfers between universities are common during the postdoc years. For men in such situations, it is common for them to take their wives along, no matter where they are pursuing postdoc. It is rare in India to find a man who will drop his job and life to move for his wife's new job. As a result, women in research drop out in huge numbers.

If we have more female professors, no female student will ever think she is not cut out for the sciences. Representation is important. Having diverse points of view at the table increases the chances of success for any project. If men and women are equal, then why not in scientific circles too? My advice to women is to never give up on their goals and dreams. Have faith in yourself, work hard, keep at it and don't let societal pressures force you to quit.

I am incredibly lucky to have become a postdoc researcher without the pressure of having to get married and 'settle down'. Yes, there were neighbours and relatives who would sometimes ask me when I would get married, but fortunately my parents never echoed their sentiments. My parents fiercely protected me from all of it. Of course, all this makes it harder for me to find a spouse who is right for me, but not for a moment do I regret my decision of investing in my career.

6

Flight Commander: Rucha Nirale

Today 12 per cent of pilots in Indian airlines are women[13]

If there was a defining point in my life, it would have to be the day I watched *Top Gun*.

I was fourteen when my brother and I saw it. After the movie, I could barely move. I was blown away. Eventually, we bought the video cassette, and I watched it at least ten times in the year 1998. There is an iconic scene in the movie where Tom Cruise races his motorbike as a MIG 29 takes off the runway. I'd never seen anything cooler in my life. Suddenly, I found myself daydreaming about becoming a fighter pilot.

Before the movie, I had dreamt of becoming many things when I grew up – schoolteacher, environmentalist, public defender and doctor, changing my mind or alternating between options every six months. But now everything else paled in comparison. On the television screen, the massively charming and good-looking Tom Cruise in his flight commander uniform struck a chord with me like nothing else had before. Suddenly, I knew what I wanted to do. Fly a plane! But I didn't want to fly just any plane, I wanted to serve my country too. I wanted to be a fighter pilot.

My maternal grandfather, Ajoba, played a huge role in shaping my worldview and personality. Ajoba was all about tough love. 'You have to do well so that you can help other people. A human being is respected based on her contributions to society and not based on her background or wealth. You must be remembered for the good you have done for others,' Ajoba repeated this to us children every summer when we visited him. So it was that I grew up with a tunnel vision of being of service to the people of my country.

Ajoba was a school principal in Nanded, Maharashtra. He had a huge collection of books; it was a dream for book lovers. As a child I never liked reading. I thought of it as a chore. But Ajoba made sure he changed how I felt about books. Ajoba would give us a set of books to read and later quiz us on what we'd learnt. Summer vacations felt like an extension of school! But gradually, I began to love books so much that reading became a habit.

My father is from a family of farmers in Bidar, Karnataka, and my mother is from a village in Maharashtra. After my father finished his technical engineering in Bidar, he was encouraged by his elder brother to move to Mumbai. My father joined MTNL as a junior technician, living at my uncle's house back then. When he had saved enough money, my father moved into a tiny, dingy, rented apartment in Powai, and soon afterwards my grandparents found him a bride. Both my parents worked themselves to the bone to give us a good childhood. They never spent anything on themselves. In fact, my parents went on their first holiday only after my father retired from work in 2009, when my brother and I were finally financially independent.

Growing up, my brother and I were opposites. He was a star at academics while I never scored more than 70 per cent marks. My brother spent most of his time brooding and studying, while I had many friends and liked being outdoors.

Thanks to Ajoba, I've always been an avid reader of newspapers. Also, in the 1990s, there was no Internet, and news came in the form of television, radio or print. As I became a teenager, any news about the army, navy or air force would catch my fancy. I would immerse myself in their full-page advertisements calling for job applicants. And once I watched *Top Gun*, my fate was sealed.

I would often tell my parents that it was my dream to join the air force. My parents thought this too was one of those passing phases, because the year before I had been determined to become a lawyer. They were sure I'd change my mind as soon as something else caught my attention. But I was steadfast in my decision. I'd always wanted to serve my country, and in what better way than by joining the air force?

My parents soon realized that I was not kidding about joining the air force after school. They were apprehensive about my decision because they'd never heard about girls in the air force. But, despite their fears, my parents didn't stop me from sitting for the air force exams. While contributing to the country and society was a prominent factor driving my career choice, I was also a thrill seeker. I didn't want to become a doctor or engineer in the military, I wanted to be a pilot. Unfortunately, I didn't clear the eyesight exam and was left heartbroken. I spent many days crying in my room.

My father then intervened with a solution to my predicament. 'If you are so bent on becoming a pilot, why don't you try civil aviation? The medical requirements for the air force and civil aviation are different.' His advice lifted my spirits. It was like going up in the air against gravity. My father and I began to research and enquire about civil aviation courses and job opportunities in the aviation sector. As luck would have it, a new college called Institute of Aviation and Aviation Safety had been established in Mumbai. It offered a BSc in aviation. I passed the written test and cleared the interview and medicals too. I was one of the four girls they picked for a class of thirty.

This was in the early 2000s, and the course fee was approximately Rs 15 lakh. Just the thought of such a large fee made me feel nervous and disillusioned. How could we afford such an exorbitant fee? To make matters worse, everyone who knew about my decision advised my parents not to send me to aviation school. 'It's a risky job.' 'Is it safe for women?' 'She'll never be home.' 'Why are you spending so much money, and that too on a girl?' 'What if she doesn't get a job after all this investment?' 'What will you do?' 'Who will marry her if she's never around?' They were bombarded with questions. It was only natural that my mother panicked. But she knew that my heart was set on flying. I was not going to back out. She told me that since I'd voluntarily chosen to pursue a difficult path, I would have to stick it out and work twice as hard to make a mark in the field. My father never wavered from the decision. Once, at a family wedding, my father lost it with some of my relatives who were going on about my career choice. 'Fine! She won't get a job,' he snapped. 'We'll lose our money. Is that the worst thing that could happen to us?' My father shut everyone up. I was so proud of him that day, and his steadfastness helped cement my courage. For the first time I realized that it doesn't matter what society dictates or says if you have the support of the people who matter most to you. My father paid part of the fees and applied for a loan for the remaining amount. He told me he had faith in me and that I could do it. There are not too many Indian parents who would resist family pressure. I am forever indebted to my parents for supporting me and allowing me to choose my future.

The aviation programme was a three-year course comprising theory classes and practical flying lessons at the flying club. Very soon into the coursework I realized that aviation was extremely hard work. If your heart's not in it, you are not going to be able to make it. My school friends would often reach out to me, telling me about the wonderful things they were doing in college – about the movies they'd watched, the road trips they'd been on and about how they were bunking classes to go to parties. Their carefree lives were in stark contrast to mine, and there were times when I felt I was missing out on life. I was an outgoing, social person, and here I was, holed up in my class studying 24/7. There were many times when I'd think, 'Yaar, everyone is chilling, why am I the only one studying like a psychopath?'

But, of course, I knew what I'd signed up for. A course in aviation isn't like a typical college course. Our schedule was divided into coursework and flying days. On coursework days I went to college at 9 a.m. and sat through the theory classes till 4 p.m. On the other days I went to the flying club early in the morning. After classes, I would go home and study uninterruptedly for another four to five hours every day. During exams my study time doubled, and burning the midnight oil became the norm. To complete the course and get a commercial pilot's licence, we had to clear five practical flying tests. Unlike other colleges, our college allowed us to sit for the exams whenever we felt ready to do so at any point during the three-year course. The course is not for people who need extensive instruction and spoon-feeding. To become a pilot, you have to be responsible, highly disciplined and self-motivated. No one's going to tell you what you need to do.

The first time I saw an airplane was also the first time I flew one. It was a Cessna 152 – a small, two-seater, propeller engine aircraft. There were butterflies in my stomach as I walked towards it. My instructor gave me a walk-through of all the external engine checks I needed to perform before take-off, and then we were inside the cockpit. All the while my heart hammered in my ears. Once inside, I strapped myself in beside my instructor. The instant I held the control column I felt a bolt of excitement shoot through me, and I knew immediately what it was – I was born to do this. I had been beating myself up about my decision to join aviation school until this point, and now, suddenly, all my worries disappeared. This was the moment of clarity I had needed. Here was my life's purpose. When you know, you just know.

We spent a few minutes performing internal checks in the cockpit, and then a message from the air control tower crackled on the radio, 'Cleared for take-off!' It was now or never. I started the aircraft and began to race it down the runway. The noise from the engines was deafening as we gathered a speed of up to 120 kilometres per hour. If you looked outside at this moment, the world seemed a blur. Most students throw up on their first day inside the cockpit, but I didn't. I loved the speed, the thrill in my stomach, and I loved the moment I was finally airborne. There is no feeling in the world that comes close to that of flying.

We went up to 4000 feet and then descended to 500 feet. We circled around a 50-foot-tall Shiva statue. I saw birds flying beneath me for the first time. The higher up you go, the more you see. I asked my instructor if we could go inside a cloud, and he said yes. As a child I thought clouds were magical and mystical. I was now inside a real cloud!

I called my parents as soon as I landed and described my experience to them in detail. I chatted non-stop with them for an hour. My parents found it hard to believe that I hadn't been afraid during the flight even for one moment.

Of course, it wasn't all thrill at the college. There were theory classes, which I hated in the beginning. But after my first flight I realized their importance. When I flew solo for the first time, I realized that there wasn't going to be an instructor around to rescue me if things went wrong. No one was going to tell me what to do, and no one was there to save me once I was up in the air. I had to do this myself. It was imperative that I knew my lessons like the back of my hand, because even a tiny mistake could mean a brutal crash. Not only was it just my life that I could endanger, but in the future I was going to be responsible for many more lives, and many people would be counting on me to keep them safe. Suddenly, the bigger picture became clear, and I realized that flying was far from just a thrilling activity; it was a serious responsibility. In that moment of realization, I grew up.

Many students dropped out from the initial set of thirty within a few months into the programme. Some realized that the course was too hard, both physically and mentally, while others didn't have the appetite for it. In the process we became a small group, and we became good friends. But there was always an undercurrent of competition colouring our friendship. Everyone wanted to pass their flying tests as quickly as possible so that they could move on to getting jobs. The coursework was demanding – we had to excel at every module or we couldn't fly. The dramatic competition that you see among pilots in movies such as *Top Gun* is for real!

Around the time of my graduation in 2005, there was suddenly a great spurt in new airlines being introduced in the market. There was IndiGo, Kingfisher, Deccan and SpiceJet. Suddenly, flying was for everyone, and it became a truly exciting time for pilots. As soon as I completed my course I received job offers from most of the airlines.

Picking an offer was a no-brainer for me. Airbus and Boeing are the two major aircraft providers in our industry. A Boeing machine offers more flexibility to pilots because it is like driving a manual gear car, whereas Airbus aircraft are highly automated, with state-of-the-art software. Automatic aircraft are easier to fly, but most pilots who want to experience the pleasure of flying prefer manual gear to automatic. My choice was made easy for me. Jet Airways had Boeing aircraft, and so I chose them.

I joined Jet as a trainee first officer. Once again, I went through a rigorous training programme, as per the company's procedures and protocols. As a trainee first officer, my job was to sit back, observe and learn procedures from my seniors. This phase of the job is called observation. After the observation phase, I had to take the simulator flying tests. A simulator is the exact lab replica of the actual aircraft. Only once I cleared this phase was I promoted to first officer. It takes two to four years, depending on your performance, before you are promoted to commander.

In 2011, I became a flight commander. I was anxious about my new position. I was twenty-six, and didn't think I was ready for such a responsibility. As a flight commander, you are the ultimate authority. You are responsible and answerable for everything that goes right or wrong while flying. I hesitated to accept the offer, but my mentor, Captain Kunal Khajuria, pushed me to go for it. 'Just go out there and figure it out. How will you ever find out whether you are ready or not if you don't try?' he said. His trust in me and his reassuring words made me take the leap. Of course, I was delighted to accept the post. All my hard work had finally paid off, and my parents were super proud of me. Also, I must add that when you see heads turn as you walk into a room in your uniform, it gives you a different kind of thrill altogether!

My first flight as a commander was from Bengaluru to Mumbai. There was light rain, the sun was setting and the sky was lit up in a hue of colours. Outside, the world looked at peace, but inside the cockpit it was a whole different story. I was beyond nervous. As soon as we landed I went to the bathroom and cried. Afterwards, the crew brought me a little cake. The day a new commander is released, the crew and first officers sign all over the commander's shirt. It's a small ritual of passing. It was midnight when I got home, and my parents were waiting for me to hear all about my first flying experience as a commander. I told my parents that I had had a great day and that I was going to get damn good at this job.

The road to becoming a commander is far from easy. Everything happens at a lightning-fast pace on board. For the first few months, I was overwhelmed by the speed of work, but gradually I got used to it. Every day I have to make countless decisions swiftly, sometimes within a second. Once, on one of my flights, a pregnant woman injured herself by falling between the seats. We were flying over the Arabian Sea at that time. I was flying from Dubai to Mangaluru. I immediately informed air control about the situation, checked if there was a doctor on board, made sure that the staff had given the woman the first aid she required and made a decision on whether I should divert the aircraft or continue to the destination – all this in a matter of minutes. Dilly-dallying is not an option.

As a pilot, you have no such thing as a fixed schedule. I am always in a different place. Sometimes I wake up in Delhi, go to bed in Abu Dhabi and end up in Thailand the next morning. I manage my sleep based on my flying schedule. If I am flying later in the night I wake up early, get a good workout, eat well and sleep in the afternoon. If I have a morning flight I then avoid sleeping in the afternoon and sleep early in the evening instead, so I can wake up early in the morning. Sometimes I get four hours of sleep before flying and clock in three more hours after landing. I have learned to make use of my schedule to my advantage. I fit my life into the day I have. I make time for family and my personal well-being in the hours I have for myself. Being fit is extremely important as a pilot. Regular tests are conducted by the airline to test our physical and mental fitness. If we don't clear even one parameter, we're not allowed to fly.

As a commander, I can never be in a bad mood as it will permeate down to my first officer, to the cabin crew and finally to the passengers. I set the tone of the plane. I don't bring personal matters with me on board because I'm aware of my immense responsibility each time I fly. I practise meditation because it brings me peace of mind and helps me stay calm. It's especially useful when I fly into a thunderstorm – the worst experience for a pilot. The slightest bit of lightning can make the most confident pilot feel nervous. Nature in a bad mood can be a frightening experience when you're in the air. Thankfully, in our training we do hours and hours of simulations of bad weather situations. But a calm disposition is a must. So I make it a point to stay calm, because if I don't then the whole crew will go bonkers.

When I was starting out as a pilot, many of my relatives ridiculed the idea of women in the cockpit. 'How long can you fly?' they'd say. 'You will get tired quickly.' 'What will happen once you get married and have children?' 'Will you still fly then?' To all those questions, my answer was always the same – if men can do it, so can I! I've flown more than 2000 flights so far. A pilot retires at sixty-five, and I want to keep going until then to prove the naysayers wrong.

Being a pilot has nothing to do with gender. When I joined the airlines, there were very few female pilots around. Today 12 per cent of all pilots in Indian airlines are women. I want to see that proportion rise to 50 per cent. It is a demanding job that takes you away from your home and personal life, but it is also exciting, lets you see the world and make interesting connections with people. The women commanders before me worked hard to pave the way for me, for us. It's now my responsibility to be an example for the next generation of women. I want to be a trailblazer. I want to show the world, and women in particular, that you can have a life even with a challenging job like this. When I took up the aviation course there was no one I knew whom I could look to for advice, so now I volunteer at schools and talk about my job so that more people, especially girls, can consider aviation as a career choice.

I want to bust the myth that women cannot be pilots or cannot have a personal life if they become one. I got married two years ago. I was sure about only one thing while deciding on my partner – he couldn't be a pilot! It's important to have some variety in life. My parents asked me if they should find me a groom. I agreed, but on one condition – he had to be right for me. I wasn't asking for much, but the man I would marry had to trust me 100 per cent, otherwise our relationship would never work. I travel all the time, going to different countries and sharing my room with other staff members. Trust was crucial. And so my parents began to connect me with eligible men. One of the men I'd been introduced to was shocked to find out how much I earned. That evening his father called mine to say they were not interested in a woman who earned more than their son! My parents and I still laugh about it. One day, my aunt introduced me to Saurabh. She gave him my number and asked him to call me. Even on our first call I could sense that he was different from the other men I had met. When we finally met in person, I just knew he was the one. He is a grounded, sweet man and, more importantly, understands the demands of my job. There is no place for ego in our relationship. My husband works in real estate and does most of the housework when I'm not there. Other people may find this unconventional, but in our family we don't even think about it.

Being a pilot is all about sacrifice. When people are holidaying and spending time with their families, I am working the hardest. I haven't been home for four consecutive Diwalis. I don't get to attend parties, weddings or spend time with my extended family. But for every six days I fly, I take two days off. This is when I catch up on rest, spend time with family, read and exercise. These two days help me relax and reset. Even the best airplanes need to reboot once in a while, and similarly, even the human body needs a reset.

As a young woman, you should consider both the pros and cons of a career choice. Not every day will offer clear skies. On some days there will be thunderstorms too. And when there is a thunderstorm, you have to find a path through the sky and stay focused on reaching your destination.

7

Brand Marketer: Ruth Sequeira

Women account for only 25 per cent of
board-level positions in publicly traded fashion
and luxury brands globally[14]

My father never wanted his children to grow up in a city. He believed children needed to grow up surrounded by nature and that they should have an active, outdoorsy lifestyle. In 1990, just before I was born, my father quit his job at a pharmaceutical company in Mumbai and decided to move to Goa for good. He sold our flat in Bandra and bought a 100-year-old Portuguese house in Saligao. My father was raised in Mumbai; however, as a child he had spent his summers in Goa with his grandparents, and he had cherished his time there.

Once we moved, my mother got a job as an English and history teacher at the nearby school, and my father worked at Mahindra & Mahindra.

Goa was a dream come true for any child. My two elder brothers, Luke and David, and I were kicked out of the house at 3 p.m. every day to go and play in the fields. Sure, we had a television at home, but it was never as exciting as being out in the sun, playing cricket or climbing trees. Moving to Goa is the greatest gift my father gave us.

Don't get me wrong. Life wasn't all smooth sailing.

Goa was underdeveloped when we were growing up. Rural life was hard for a city-bred person like my mother. We didn't have running water till I was nine; we had to fetch water from the well next door every day. Goan public transport in those days was practically non-existent.

Talking about my father's death has never been easy. Soon after we'd moved to Goa, my father developed a drinking problem. He tried to but couldn't give up alcohol. He was gravely ill for a couple of months before he passed away from kidney failure. Even though we knew his death was imminent, it came as a massive blow to us. One night my mother took him to the hospital and she came back alone. The next morning we woke up to a lot of noise and commotion in our house. It was only when I saw my mother crying that I realized what had happened. She told us he wasn't coming home again.

My father died one day before my tenth birthday. He had promised me a bicycle because my current one was now too small for me. He had been saving money for my bicycle, and my mother found the bundle of notes for it in his shirt pocket. She immediately bought me the bicycle he'd promised. She knew it would have made him happy. And even though we were in mourning, she hosted a dinner for the family.

Of course, there was gossip in the village. Why aren't they mourning? Why are her children wearing bright colours during the mourning period? My mother took a lot of bullets for us in those days. She stood her ground and let us live as my father would have wanted us to.

Despite outward appearances, we grieved for my father in our own ways. My mother found solace in church and social work. She threw open our house to people in need – women who'd been beaten by their drunk husbands or migrants who had just arrived in Goa looking for a job. There were many instances when we would wake up to random strangers sleeping in our house. People from all classes of society found refuge in our home. We didn't have much ourselves, but that never stopped my mother from feeding the hungry and sheltering those in need.

We had to grow up immediately after my father's death – one day we woke up and everything had changed. We were a single-income family. My mother had three children to support. We owned the house, so at least we had all the basic amenities, but we had to rough it out to just get by. My mother spent most of her earnings on our education. I didn't have toys or outings like other children. My mother started a catering business to supplement her teacher's salary. She would take orders for pickles and baked goods. My eldest brother, Luke, was the head of packaging and transport. David and I would do the prep work and cleaning. It took up all our time, but we had to stick it out. At home, we took turns to wash the dishes and clean up. We always helped our mother out in the kitchen. For the longest time, I didn't realize that girls around the country were treated differently from boys, because at home everybody took turns to do chores.

My mother continues working to this day – she volunteers with a group that focuses on educating prisoners, she teaches at a school, and she also heads a group that helps widows seek empowerment. Having raised three kids all by herself as a single mother, she is passionate about the last cause.

I coped with my father's death in another way: I found grief. Being the youngest, I had been my father's favourite. He would drop me to and pick me up from school every day. I remember standing in front of him on his Vespa as he drove me around Saligao; it was such a thrill. He encouraged me to read and took a keen interest in expanding my vocabulary. When he died, I would often tell my mother that I didn't want to live any more, that I wanted to be with my father in heaven. Worried about my state of mind, my mother had me transferred to the school where she taught. She wanted to keep an eye on me. School can be a difficult place for many children, and more so if you are a teacher's kid. As a teacher's child, I faced the wrath of the other students. There was a group of six girls who made my life miserable at school. They teased me and didn't let the other girls in class talk to me. Those were some of the hardest days of my life.

Only time can heal you from an emotional tragedy. It took me about three years to get over my father's death. But, in a way, his death brought our family closer. We developed a deeper bond with each other. We ploughed through the hard times and came out of them stronger and more compassionate. We don't take anything for granted any more. My brothers are the first people I call when I'm going through tough times. I know that if anything goes wrong I'll always have my family's support and strength backing me.

I was always an average student at school, scoring in the 70–75 per cent range. But I studied to learn and understand, not to score marks. My eldest brother, Luke, who is five years older than me, had to fill the void my father left. He was always interested in business and entrepreneurship. He would read autobiographies and business books, and got me started on them young. At school, when all my friends were reading Harry Potter, I was reading *Tipping Point* by Malcolm Gladwell and *The World Is Flat* by Thomas L. Friedman. So I felt I had a head start in life! I read the Potter series too (how could you not?!), but I guess I felt older than my peers because of my brother's influence.

I joined one of the top colleges in Goa to study mass communication for my undergraduate degree. Within two days of the course, I realized it was not meant for me. I felt a deep unrest. I enquired about other marketing and advertising courses, and someone suggested Sophia College in Mumbai. The next thing I knew, I was on a bus to maximum city. When I got there, the city was flooded because of the monsoon, and I had to wade through knee-high water to get to the college. The department head informed me that I was late for admissions. The classes were full, but she assured me that if any seats opened up they would contact me. The bus ride back to Goa was a miserable one; I cried all the way home because I was desperate for a better education option. Fortunately, my luck turned, and a week later Sophia called to say they could take me in.

My mother gave me Rs 2000 every month as pocket money. I had to manage all my expenses within that amount. In Mumbai, I saw outrageously rich people for the first time. There were students who would come to college in a Mercedes car and spend Rs 2000 on a meal – my budget for the whole month! I was the only student in college without a laptop too. For all my assignments I used the one computer available in the lab. I had to figure out when that one computer would be available and organize the rest of my schedule accordingly. This helped me become a disciplined and resourceful person.

Sophia College gave me the education I had craved in Goa. I studied hard, worked on all my assignments and got good grades. I held multiple leadership positions as class representative, hostel secretary and college general secretary. I also won the student of the year award. Finally, I was coming into my own.

I was the first person in my family who applied for a corporate job. My brother, Luke, had started an online business at eighteen, while David chose to pursue higher education. For the first time, I felt lost. My brothers were usually the people I consulted on all my major life decisions, but in this case they couldn't help me because they had no experience in the matter. I blindly went into the corporate world. It took me three short stints with different companies before I found my dream job.

I had moved to Chennai for one of my jobs. I was working as a digital marketing manager for a health foods company. Chennai was a good break from Mumbai, but I also found it hard to settle in, given the language barrier. One day, a friend who was applying to Hidesign – India's leading luxury leather accessories brand with a presence in over twenty-three countries – asked me to send in my CV too. I'd heard a lot about Hidesign and was aware of their beautiful products, but I could never afford any of them. My friend's suggestion piqued my interest, and I immediately called their HR department. They asked me to come in for an interview over the weekend. I bought a bus ticket for Rs 83 to Puducherry, and when I got there I stayed at Puducherry University with a friend of a friend! I had no money for fancy travel or for a hotel stay.

Imagine my disappointment then, when during the interview I found that the HR at Hidesign had got my résumé mixed up with someone else's! They had called me by mistake! I was both devastated and infuriated. I had come all the way from Chennai for this interview. As I was about to leave the room, Dilip Kapur, the founder and president of the company, asked me if I'd consider a different profile based in Mumbai. He'd been impressed with our meeting and all the extracurriculars I'd been a part of in college. He asked me if I would be interested in joining their retail operations team because that was the only role they had open. I had never done sales or operations before. This was a whole new territory, but I didn't hesitate. I took the offer. I was the youngest retail manager Hidesign had ever hired. I was to start immediately in the Mumbai office.

A couple of months after I took up the role in Mumbai, the person who oversaw the Mumbai team left on a maternity break. Suddenly, all the Mumbai operations were left to me and another colleague. I was only twenty-two, and there I was heading the team of a major luxury brand! Usually, people who had roles like mine had done their postgraduation and had some relevant work experience. I had neither, except for the drive and hunger to learn and perform. It was overwhelming, but instead of feeling anxious I decided to view it as a challenge. I jumped into operations from day one! I learnt more in those first few months than I had all through school and college. I pushed myself to pick up new areas of work and learn the ropes. I found myself managing four top stores in the city. My schedule was loaded. I would leave home at 6 a.m. and be back only by 11 p.m. Weekends were full working days because that's when most people shop.

After a year and a half I was promoted – I was given ownership of four retail stores and twenty-two department stores in Hyderabad and one store in Goa. I was a twenty-three-year-old who was doing a thirty-five-year old's job. Our Hyderabad outlets were in bad shape because of mismanagement and theft. The company sent me there to clean up the mess. When I showed up at the Hyderabad outlet, no one could understand why a young person like me was telling them what to do. It wasn't pleasant. In a year's time, I had to fire ninety-eight people and rebuild the team from scratch.

Even though I was capable for my role, my heart lay in digital marketing and brand communications. I spoke to Dilip, and he happily agreed to give me a suitable role. And so I moved to the Puducherry headquarters of Hidesign for good.

I have been leading brand communications and digital marketing for Hidesign since March 2015. Any written communication from Hidesign has to be approved by me. I handled some of their biggest collaborations, such as the ones with Disney and Kalki Koechlin. I understand the company's values to the core, so now I also train store staff in communication and brand ethos. Every time we open a store at a new location, I'm always there to train the staff. My job has taken me to many countries and, in the process, travel has become a passion. You could call me a workaholic, but I see it differently. I work for work's sake. I believe that whatever you do, you should do well and seek perfection. Hidesign as a brand stands for high-quality craftsmanship, which aligns perfectly with my ethos. One of the best ways to grow in a job or at a company is to say yes to all the challenges that are thrown at you. If you prove yourself in those areas, you can build trust with the leadership, which is really what I did during my time at Hidesign.

After passing out of college, my friends and I had made a short trip to Puducherry on a minimal budget to celebrate our graduation milestone. Little did I know that

I would eventually live in Puducherry. Life in Puducherry suits me. I live alone in a small apartment in the French colony. I love the slow pace and the beauty I'm surrounded by. In a way, it reminds me of my childhood. I am immensely grateful that I've been given the opportunity to have a high-flying corporate job without the bustle of being in a big city. I either walk or cycle to work. I go running on the beach, do yoga and take French classes. I am part of the organizing committee of the Puducherry Heritage Festival and Fair Trade Puducherry–Auroville. It's important to be part of meaningful initiatives outside work too and build a community of people around you who are doers.

If you see how savvy I am with digital marketing and building brand communications online, you'd never guess that I went through college without a laptop. Sometimes it's the constraints that define us and push us to do bigger things. I take pride in overcoming obstacles and excelling at my career.

A career choice is often not clear at the beginning. We must try different things and experiment with jobs before we settle on something. You've got to stumble a little before you figure what drives you, or what makes you happy, or what you can *potentially* be good at. It took me too some time to do that. But the detours along the way were absolutely essential, and now, looking back, it was all worth it.

8

Photographer: Shravya Kag

Globally, only 20 per cent of photojournalists are women[15]

I spent the first twenty-one years of my life living with my parents in Vijayawada, Andhra Pradesh. My life was cocooned in a typical Telugu upbringing. And of course my parents wanted me to become an engineer, like all good Telugu children. Even in my wildest dreams I never thought I would one day become a cutting-edge photographer.

The only reason I got good grades at school was that my mother pushed me very hard at academics. It was more her efforts than mine that paid off when the results were declared. But when I became an adolescent I began to resist her, and gradually my grades began to slip. No longer was I first in class. To be frank, I was okay with where I stood.

After school, I sat for the engineering entrance exams, just like all the other neighbourhood children. The year was 2007. You see, engineering is the field that parents most want their children to get into. Engineering is the standard path. If you are a respectable Telugu child, you pursued engineering, went to the United States for a master's programme or did an MBA. Where I come from, the average kid does not deviate from this path because he or she usually does not know of any other. This is what our parents impressed upon us. The humanities were for below-average students. Passion? Interest? What is that? None of that mattered. Back then, I too didn't know any better, so I followed the path that had been laid out for us.

It wasn't a surprise then when I ended up with a terrible rank in the local state engineering entrance exam. The college that would take me was right next to our house, but it would not take me for the coveted computer science; it accepted my admission for mechanical engineering. To be honest, I didn't care. I was okay with anything. I was just relieved that exam season was behind me. I went for a week-long holiday to our relatives' in Hyderabad, but when I came back I was in for a shock.

The president of the engineering college had convinced my parents that electrical engineering was better for my future than mechanical engineering. My anxious parents had agreed, and had paid a donation for my admission – a common demand at most engineering colleges. Their hasty decision made me stop and think for the first time in my life. It seemed my parents cared more about my future than I did myself. They were the only reason I was doing engineering. I had no idea what I wanted to do with my life. I was just following the herd. I hated the fact that my parents had spent extra money on something that I myself was unsure of.

Engineering was a disaster for me at every level. For

the first time ever, I failed a subject. Failure can be a big reality check. Humiliation took hold of me. How could I tell my parents about my college results? How could I face them? I threw myself into my studies, working through the night, spending every free moment trying to grasp a subject I had zero interest in. Gradually, I fared better. So much so that I began to help my peers with their queries and weaknesses. But despite my progress my heart was not in the subject.

While I was relieved that I was no longer failing exams, deep down I was dissatisfied, restless and unhappy. I knew I couldn't carry on this charade for too long. I considered dropping out, but I didn't have the courage to suggest that to my parents. How could I let them down? I chose the next best option, and spoke to my older brother about the turmoil I was going through. My brother was always the studious type, excelling at academics. I wasn't surprised by what he told me. 'Don't worry too much. You can make this work. It will all be okay.'

Obviously, he couldn't understand what I was going through. Listening to him, I had a moment of realization – he was wrong. I was on the wrong path. I hated engineering. No amount of external validation was now going to make a difference. Suddenly, the road ahead became crystal clear. Even though I didn't know what I wanted to do, I knew one thing for sure – I was wasting my time in engineering.

Yet, I didn't do anything about my situation! I made it all the way to the final year, right up to campus placements. And before I knew it I began to prepare for the CAT exams so that I could get into an MBA programme, just like everybody else again. I should have known how to make better choices by then, since the last time that I followed the standard path it had turned out to be a disastrous experience. One day, my brother, who knew I was miserable doing this, sat me down for a talk. 'Do you see a career for yourself as an electrical engineer? Or would you enjoy working at a company like Infosys, TCS?' The answer to both his questions was a resounding 'no'. The very thought of these options made me sick to the gut.

And then I took my first small step. I broke away from the standard path. I didn't turn up for the campus placements.

Everyone around me thought I'd gone mad. 'Don't you want a job?' they asked. None of my peers could understand my decision. My parents didn't say anything to me because they thought I was gunning for an MBA.

Suddenly, I began to question other things too. Why was I preparing for an MBA? Why should I take up MBA? Was I even interested in it or was I blindly following the set rules again? If not an MBA, then what? What did I like? What would I enjoy doing? These questions flooded me every waking moment. And then, one day, I remembered my childhood friend Nikhilesh.

Nikhilesh was studying film-making in Chennai. When he came home for the summers, we would hang out together. He was working on a short film project during the holidays and needed a helping hand. I assisted him because I didn't have anything better to do, and I thought his film project was interesting. He noticed that I had an artistic point of view and that the simple photos I took on my phone were pretty good. He taught me how to use his DSLR camera. He always said to me, 'Shravya, if you want to get into photography, the time is right now.' My journey into the world of photography began with a strong push from Nikhilesh.

So, there I was, a ball of confusion, and I couldn't help but think of Nikhilesh's words. Could I do it? Was photography my calling? The voice in my head was telling me to go for it. But how would my parents react to such a bizarre decision? From engineering to photography? They'd think I'd gone mad! The very thought of telling them about it made my heartbeat quicken. It would be both an exciting and terrifying experience.

A week later, a friend asked me to check Nikhilesh's Facebook page as something did not seem quite right. When I did, I was stumped to see a number of Rest in Peace messages on his wall. Nikhilesh had died in a train accident. This was the first time someone close to me had died. My mind raced with memories of all the times we'd spent together. I couldn't move for an entire day. I lay on my bed, gazing aimlessly at the ceiling. I couldn't get over my friend's sudden death and also how unpredictable our lives were. Perhaps it was Nikhilesh's death that propelled me to pursue my passions with a vengeance, or maybe it was not. I didn't even get to see the final version of the short film he had been making. His death left a deep scar in me. And now, the fear of not trying out something I could excel in and thrive on was more pressing than the fear of not conforming to the norm.

I finally mustered up the courage to speak to my mother about my nagging desire to pursue a master's in broadcast communications. It turned out she hadn't been blind to my dissatisfaction and unrest through my engineering years. As a parent, she didn't want me to be unhappy. She told me she would stand by my choice. Her assurance meant the world to me. I then immediately applied for a course which taught a mix of photography, scriptwriting, videography and sound mixing in Chennai.

I planned to stay with my great-grandmother in Chennai. I thought it would be like moving from one home to another. My mother accompanied me to Chennai to help me settle in. I was excited about what lay ahead. But as soon as my mother left I was miserably homesick. This was the first time I'd been away from home, and it unsettled me. I cried every night. My life had been so protected until now that I'd never realized what the real world was about.

I went home on the very first weekend. Everyone made fun of how helpless I was. I was a joke. It was easy back home, because I knew everyone and how things worked. I'd always had many friends and had been the life of the party. In Chennai, I realized that I wasn't comfortable in big groups. On the first day of class we had an ice-breaker session. Everyone had to introduce themselves, after which informal conversation would follow. I found it hard to speak, and when I did I spoke in an unnatural, measured way. This continued for a while. A friend pointed out to me that I opened up to her only when I was alone with her. It was true; I had very few friends because I never reached out to people. I thought hard about my behaviour and realized that I was an introvert! I discovered many such things about myself during my first year in Chennai.

I threw myself into my work. I made a commitment to myself that Chennai wouldn't be a repeat of my disastrous engineering years. I was going to gain real experience and find out what I was good at and could make money from. I volunteered to work for a recording studio that also made documentaries and indie films. Every day after class I would diligently show up at the studio and assist there in every capacity. I took photographs and helped with the audio and sound mixing for the ads and documentaries. I was shamelessly persistent, asking the studio for any work they could give me, and soon the studio realized they couldn't get rid of me! I would show up no matter what. So they gave me the opportunity to be the chief photographer for their music festival. However, I wasn't making any money from all this. But I didn't let that deter me; I was determined to figure out a path where I would shine and thrive professionally. This was my single-minded goal.

I topped my class the first year, which felt amazing. Nobody had forced me to excel. It was completely my choice. My experience in Chennai was in stark contrast to my engineering years.

Eventually, I worked on a movie set, where I was the behind-the-scenes photographer. They used my photos on the movie posters for the launch of the film, which was a big high for me. When there were no official gigs, I found myself spending hours on photography-related work. I began to love taking photographs of people, roads, buildings and monuments, and would edit my pictures through the night. When I wasn't shooting, I voraciously read books and blogs on photography. I was inspired and moved by the work of documentary photographers such as Vivian Maier, Elliott Erwitt, Raghubir Singh and David Alan Harvey. I spent hours studying the technical composition of their photographs. I spent 90 per cent of my day working on photography, and I found that I was immensely happy and satisfied doing so. By the end of my coursework in Chennai, it was obvious to me and to everyone else around me that photography was indeed my future. So now that I had that figured out, what were my job plans? How could I start earning money?

During this time my parents received a marriage proposal for me from a rich family in Hyderabad. The prospective groom was well settled and travelled often on work. 'You could travel with him and take pictures,' my mother told me encouragingly. I was aghast. There I was trying to figure out my career, and my parents wanted me to get married to a stranger! I vehemently refused, telling my parents that I wanted to be financially independent before I got married. My parents were distraught by my refusal. They couldn't understand why I was turning down such a good match.

'We have to fulfil our responsibilities.' 'You are twenty-three years old, and old enough to get married.' 'He has the perfect life and a great job.' 'You'll have the perfect life with him.' 'What if you're making a mistake by not considering this option?'

The exhortations were endless, but I stood my ground. I wasn't going to get married. That was when one of our family friends interjected. She told my parents that I was too young to make important decisions and it was their right as parents *to make the decision for me*. She went on to warn them that they were making a big mistake in letting me voice my opinions. That was the last straw that broke the camel's back. I flipped out!

In India, your marriage is somehow everyone else's business. People don't understand boundaries. I felt violated that someone who didn't know anything about me thought she had the right to dictate the direction of my life. I refused to speak to my parents for three days. I didn't eat anything. My parents ultimately gave in to my decision.

After I finished my course I moved back to Vijayawada to set up a photography business with a friend. We began with photography for a few weddings in the friends and family circuit. Gradually, strangers started reaching out to us because of our Facebook page. It took a while, but soon the gigs and the pay got bigger. Suddenly, I was shooting events outside my home town and was shuttling between Vijayawada and Hyderabad. Wedding photography is a lucrative business, and my partner and I began making enough money to see us through two to three months after just a week's work.

Just as the pieces of my once scattered life were falling into place, my father's began to unravel. His business fell apart, and he decided to sell our house. We had spent our entire childhood there, and every memory I had was connected to our home. We were devastated. Losing our home broke my heart.

Around the same time, I was advised by my uncle to look up photography courses in New York to broaden my horizons and think globally. His belief in my talent was flattering. 'Why confine yourself to just wedding gigs? Think bigger!' He suggested that I look up the School of Visual Arts in New York. One of their professors had started the photography blog of *The New York Times*, which I loved. At first it seemed like a ridiculous idea. My father was going through a financial crisis, we'd just sold our house, and there was my uncle encouraging me to get an advanced degree in a fringe subject like photography.

But life has a sneaky way of working out. As the days passed, I couldn't get my uncle's suggestion out of my mind. I tried to rationalize and convince myself about why I shouldn't pursue an advanced degree. But my uncle had already planted the seed of an outrageous idea in me, and soon it grew, blossoming into a million possibilities and opportunities. It began to make sense. Why shouldn't I think bigger? If I was committed to my craft, I owed it to myself to invest in it. Also, I'd always dreamed about New York. Who doesn't, right? It is the place to strike gold. It could offer me everything – the best education, mentors and business opportunities if I was dedicated and pushed myself. I spent many sleepless nights mulling over the idea.

That summer I visited my brother, who had moved to the US (you see, my brother turned out to be a good Telugu boy who finished engineering, went to the US for his master's, finished his CFA and got a job there), and pursued a short summer course in New York. I was blown away by the sheer range of opportunities the city offered. Having tested the waters, I came back to India and applied to schools in New York.

I only told my parents about New York when I had my confirmation letter from the School of Visual Arts in New York in the bag. My parents were shocked by the news, which was a fair reaction, considering I had sprung it on them without any warning. There was the issue of how we'd finance my studies too. After a lot of discussion and debate, we figured out a way to fund my studies with my savings and help from extended family.

I'd once thought moving to Chennai was a hard step, but I wasn't at all prepared for what New York had in store for me. The first few months of 2016 in New York were difficult. I couldn't follow what people were saying, and they could not understand my accent of English either. On my first day of college, a classmate, who had a thick

Southern accent, asked me for directions. I misunderstood her and pointed her in the wrong direction! She was very angry with me and it led to a hiccup between us. This episode triggered all my insecurities about dealing with people. The coursework was equally overwhelming and hectic. My new schedule wasn't anything like what it had been in Chennai. I was studying or working every waking minute of the day. All I did was go to class, work on my projects and, finally, when I was exhausted, crash on my brother's couch. I'd never thought one day could be so long!

There weren't any Indians in my class, and I found that disconcerting initially. But in hindsight I'm grateful for that because it allowed me to meet different people who were driven and passionate about what they did. I slowly had a community of inspiring people to hang out with. It took me a few months to find my momentum. New York pushed me out of my comfort zone and made me understand and harness my latent potential in a way I could've never done had I stayed home.

For the final semester thesis I chose to tell the stories of New York musicians who played in the subway. My thesis challenged the assumption that these musicians were usually poor or didn't have jobs. I met Harvard Business School and Berkeley graduates, professors from the prestigious Juilliard School and many others who played music for free in the subways. They were successful people who played music because they loved it and wanted to share their music with the world. My photo series focused on how empty and lifeless the subways would be without these musicians.

New York is majestic. It throbs with energy, talent and ideas. It gives you the freedom to pursue your dream and be who you are. For example, while growing up I was insecure about the way I looked. Straight hair is seen as a norm of standard beauty, but I had thick, curly hair, which I'd always straightened. In New York I gained confidence about my passions, my work and my life purpose, and this changed the relationship I had with myself. I began to look at my own body differently. Finally, I was comfortable in my own skin. I stopped straightening my hair, stopped thinking about what I looked like to other people. And now I always get told how attractive I am! They tell me that my curly hair is fantastic. I realized that people respond better to you if you are comfortable with yourself.

Of course, you've got to be very self-motivated and independent to live in a city like New York, because no one else is going to push you. Everyone here hustles all the time to make things work. I came from a slow work culture, so I had to rewire my mindset to make a difference here. During my years of studying and working in India, I used to take an afternoon nap every day. Here, it's unthinkable to do that! I work most of the time, and after that I network.

Around the time I finished my course, the renowned *National Geographic* journalist Ira Block, who had discovered my work, got in touch with me about a job. Ira was one of the first few photographers who had extensively documented the North Pole. He is highly respected in photography circles for his work on indigenous peoples from various parts of the world. I was flattered when he reached out to me, and I accepted the offer immediately. Ira Block travels extensively, and I assist him at his studio once he's back from his travels. I work with him three or four times a week, and I am covered financially for the month. On the other days of the week I work on my freelance projects or on my blog. Working with Ira changed the way I thought about photography. I learnt how a simple photo can influence the world. I realized the importance of documentation, and how photographs stand as evidence in an ever-changing world. Ira's work on Incan mummies in Peru showed the world human remains and artefacts from 500 years ago. His portraiture of 9/11 survivors showcased human pain and endurance. Today, my approach to photography is different because of my time under his tutelage. I am deliberate, intentional and conscious about my work. I've also developed the confidence to showcase my work at photography exhibitions in New York. Last year, my work was selected to be displayed alongside that of established photographers such as Donna Ferrato and Ron Haviv. That day I celebrated by going to my favourite spot in New York – a quiet space from where you can see the Brooklyn Bridge and the Manhattan skyline.

In 2017, I was shortlisted for the prestigious Sony World Photography Award. The news was covered by many Telugu newspapers too. My mother's friends congratulated her, telling her that Indian society needs more parents like her and my father, who allow their children to pursue their own dreams. She was proud of my achievements, and this external validation meant that she's no longer worried about my not getting married!

Sometimes I think about my stubborn refusal to marry during my twenties and smile. I'm so grateful I got to live my twenties as a single woman. Perhaps if I'd married I would never had such rich life experiences. Not marrying may not be everyone's cup of tea, but it was mine. Just the way engineering wasn't mine. I chose the unknown path, and it's led me to places I never in my wildest dreams thought I'd visit. Now I want to travel the world and let photography open me up to new places and people. Photography preserves history for future generations, and it's my privilege to be able to contribute what little I can manage to the bigger narrative.

9

Scientist: Nishma Dahal

Only 14 per cent researchers in India are women[16]

I am a mountain child. I have always understood the importance of nature's bounty and have been grateful for it. How could I not be when I've seen both nature's majesty and wrath? Everything I am is a result of that awareness.

I grew up in a small town called Soreng in west Sikkim, where the night skies were clear and star-sprinkled, the air cool and clean, and where the silhouette of the great mountains, our guardians, loomed all around us. Life in the mountains is simple. We had a fixed routine – waking up at 6 a.m., getting ready for school, and breakfasting on dal, chawal and sabzi before heading out. After school there would be tea and gossip with family and friends. There wasn't much to do in our small town. Watching movies, going out for coffee or shopping were non-existent activities. Sometimes, in the evenings, we would go for long walks, usually to Timburbong, our ancestral village, which was three kilometres away. In high school, I would trek in the nearby forests with my classmates. Entertainment for us was all about immersion in nature.

It was hard for my family to make ends meet. My parents struggled to pay our school fees. My mother never told us about any of it at that time. But once I became a teenager she would tell me about their financial struggles. My parents were primary school teachers. They rented out part of the house to tourists and students. In our parts this was the most common form of income or income supplement. As a result, I grew up surrounded by many different people. Our house had three small rooms, one of which was always on rent. When my parents had enough savings they added another storey to the building. Today my parents rent out two rooms. But even though our house was small and cramped, I loved it. From our window we could see Darjeeling and the hills – a sight I never tired of.

My school was built only three years before I enrolled there. It was a ramshackle, temporary structure, which was replaced by a concrete building only when I was in class six. It may seem strange to you, but we were lucky to even have a school in our town. My friends from the neighbouring villages didn't have even this basic amenity. For them, getting to school every day involved a long journey. So when we were in class ten, three of my school friends stayed at our house as paying guests to study and to sit for the exams. It was much easier than commuting every day.

I grew up fascinated by biology, because it dealt with things I encountered every day. What is the body made up of? What happens to the food we eat? How does the process of digestion work? What are the specific functions of each body part? Why is a leaf green in colour? How does pollination happen? Even as a young girl I was amazed by the workings of nature and how every little organism in it has a role to play. Nothing happens at random.

When I was about to finish school I began to grow anxious about where I'd study next. We did not have access to the Internet at our home. The only way we found out about colleges and courses was through our seniors who were already pursuing higher education. We were limited by what we knew, whom we knew and what we could access. My parents and I spoke to some of my school seniors, and they recommended that I look up colleges in Bengaluru. And that's how I found the Ramaiah Institute of Technology. When I finished school in 2005, I moved to Bengaluru to study biotechnology.

Moving to a big city was difficult at first. You see, people in the mountains are simple folk; I wasn't used to the pace and wiles of modernity. I stayed at a private hostel, where I had to share a room with a girl from Delhi. My parents had ingrained in me the values of cleanliness and order. My roommate, on the other hand, was messy, and every time I arranged her things she would lose it with me for touching her belongings. I was confused about her behaviour; I couldn't understand why she got upset with me for helping her. It took me a while to understand the concept of personal space. I'd grown up in a society where we didn't even think about things like that. We shared everything we had. Plus, we were not well off; to be able to afford privacy is a luxury. My family lived together in a small house, where we shared everything with each other; there was no concept of personal space. It took me a long time to realize that people from big cities are just different. They are much more confident, independent, blunt and open about their feelings. It took me a lot of conditioning and unlearning to get used to the ways of the city.

I was chronically homesick. I was painfully shy and couldn't make friends. Also, I didn't have the money to spend time outside the hostel or to explore the city. There were many times when I wanted to quit and go back to Sikkim, but then I would think about the money my parents had spent on my college fees, and that was motivation enough for me to stay and continue my education. I felt a deep sense of responsibility towards my parents.

Ragging was another big problem. Stalkers would send horrendous SMSs. They would follow me, and that ultimately prompted me to change hostels. I started carrying pepper spray. This was a terrible state of affairs. I am really tiny and I am from north-east India, both of which make me an easy target for harassment by men. I don't know how we can change this situation for girls, but it's extremely saddening. Things got better for me after I moved in with my elder sister who had taken up a job in Bengaluru.

The only thing I was sure about when I was completing my graduation was that I did not want a nine-to-five job. I wanted to be in research, where I would be able to do some original thinking and meaningful work. I cold-emailed many professors from the Indian Institute of Science (IISc), but they did not have any open positions in my field. One of the professors from IISc mentioned that the National Centre for Biological Sciences (NCBS) had many projects that I could consider. I had never heard of NCBS before this, so I immediately looked it up. NCBS is a premier research institute for biological sciences under the Tata Institute of Fundamental Research. I went through their website and was amazed by their work. I found out that they were conducting a massive project in Sikkim, and suddenly I began to feel excited about my prospects.

The Sikkim project on evolutionary biology was being conducted by Dr Uma Ramakrishnan, who conducts research in the field of ecology and evolution in animals. Her topic – the study of animals of high-altitude regions – naturally fascinated me. I was keen to work with her. One day, I turned up at her office in Bengaluru without writing to her or calling her in advance. Of course, Dr Ramakrishnan was surprised to find me there and asked me to come back another day. She probably thought I wouldn't show up again. But I did. At that point she was convinced that I was genuinely interested in her project. She asked me to assist one of her PhD students, who gave me a ton of research papers to read. It was my first time reading research work, and I was determined to submit a good report. I spent days and nights at the lab poring over the papers. Eventually, Dr Ramakrishnan took a chance with me.

Dr Ramakrishnan gives her students the freedom to choose their projects. She believes in independent thought. Right from the start I was clear that I wanted lab work because it doesn't involve being on the road, going out into the wild to trap animals to collect samples for research. I'd always lived a protected life and thought I wasn't cut out for the field. There was also the perception that fieldwork is masculine, and sadly, I fell into that trap.

At NCBS, I read everything I could lay my hands on, immersing myself in all kinds of papers. Soon I realized that I was fascinated by evolution, especially animal evolution in high-altitude mountainous regions, where climate fluctuations and mountain uplift have a role in shaping the current diversity of species. I wanted to study how all this impacted species in the Himalayas. I chose to study the pika – a small mammal found exclusively in high-altitude regions. Kin to the rabbit and hare, though with shorter ears, it usually has a furry, light brown coat and a rounded appearance.

The questions I was trying to answer through my research were fundamental. What species of pikas exist today? How are they distributed along the Himalayas, where the habitat changes so drastically along the elevation gradient? How have they evolved over time? How did climatic fluctuations in the past impact this species? If you understand how climatic fluctuations affect animals, you can also extrapolate from that and predict how they will respond to future climate change. Pikas live in a cold environment, and as the world is getting hotter, they may soon lose their habitat. I went headlong into research without any expectations, but soon I fell in love with the challenge of scientific reasoning and the independence that it provides. But sooner or later I had to venture into fieldwork. I couldn't hide out in the lab forever.

Fieldwork in high-altitude regions is extremely challenging. First, the weather allows you only two to three months out in the field. That meant I had to plan my trips down to the tiniest detail. My job was to find the pikas, trap them and then conduct my study. And the way to find an elusive animal is to first look for their poop! I spent weeks just collecting their faecal pellets, in the hope that I could study their DNA. Back in Bengaluru, I realized that the pellets can only give you limited information as they are a degraded source of DNA. If I had to get the pika's DNA intact, I'd have to catch the animal itself. It was necessary for me to get their tissue samples.

Pikas are lightning quick and shy. Even though they are abundant in the areas where they are found, as they live in groups, catching them is another story altogether. One of my colleagues at NCBS was working on rodents. She taught me everything about how to set up traps, what locations to set them in, what signs to look for, and the types of food that can be used to attract pikas. For somebody who was terrified of rats, I had made tremendous progress!

Our pika-catching crew comprised a field assistant, a group of local people and me. We'd spend all day walking through the mountain forests with our metal traps looking for the animals. Since I grew up in a high-altitude region, I fared well, having been used to walking great distances. Of course, sometimes after a day's work, with no success in sight, I'd lament to Dr Ramakrishnan that I had probably taken up the wrong project. But Dr Ramakrishnan would always push me to try harder.

After months passed with no sightings, I began to experiment with the traps. I stopped changing my trap locations, leaving them in the same place for three or four days. I hoped the pikas would grow comfortable with the foreign object. I started pitching my tent near the trapping site and checking the traps at night. I also started experimenting with the kind of food I left in the traps. I started with peanut butter, but over time I learned that apples, carrots and local vegetation worked better. Trapping animals can test your patience. It is an immensely boring and uncertain task. My first expedition in the Himalayas was in 2011, and I caught a pika only two years later.

Fieldwork is not for the faint-hearted, especially if you're up against nature. Sometimes you don't get to bathe for two or three weeks at a stretch. At other times you may run out of food. The living conditions are usually tough as hell, and you've got to do all the work yourself – carrying and setting up your own tents, carrying all the food you need for the duration of the trip, and collecting dried vegetation, twigs and yak dung for fire at night. You have to defecate in the open as there are no toilets. There have been countless times when I felt disillusioned and depressed. But I couldn't abandon my research, so the next morning I'd wake up and soldier on. I never told my parents where I was going on my expeditions! I felt it would make them unnecessarily anxious. Before my trips I would give them a heads-up, telling them I would be away for two to three months and that I would not have access to the phone or Internet.

Every year the expeditions I conducted came with their unique challenges. West Sikkim was the most difficult expedition I had conducted. The forests are dense and dark, and there are no roads. Every leg of the journey was on foot. We had hired a yak to carry our luggage – over 60 kg of food, clothes, traps, food for pikas and drinking water – to our camping station at Somitey Lake located inside Kanchenjunga National Park. We started walking from a small village called Yuksom. It took us four days to reach Somitey Lake. The plan was to work at Somitey for four days and go downhill to a place called Dzongri. We asked the yak owner to come back to fetch us in four days. On the very first night there was a massive snowstorm. Our tents were crushed under the snow and we had to take shelter under a huge rock. The snowstorm continued unabated for three nights, and our team waited it out under the rock. I began to worry for our lives. Things came to such a head that my crew and I decided to walk down to a lower-altitude region to seek safety. The yak owner didn't show up as promised. We were helpless and had to carry all the luggage ourselves. Imagine walking downhill, 20 kg on your back and knee-deep in snow, and all the while a snowstorm raging around you! It was a nightmare.

Once, while trekking through the Annapurna ranges in 2012, we ran out of food. And we came across a house in the middle of nowhere. Even though the family that lived there was destitute, they offered us food and shelter. Before leaving I tried to give them some money, but they vehemently refused it. I didn't know how to persuade them to take the money without offending them.

According to the biodiversity laws, you are not allowed to carry tissue samples across borders. So in 2013 I had to stay back in Nepal to finish my lab work on the animal tissues I had collected from there. It was hard to get any permits in Nepal. They did not have many rules to begin with and, in my case, they were confused because I could speak the Nepali language despite being an Indian citizen. A vast majority of the people in Sikkim can speak Nepali; we migrated from Nepal generations ago when Sikkim was still an independent country. I had to constantly show up at the ministry and beg them to give me the permissions needed to finish my research. They finally said yes. Persistence is a skill I work on every day in this field of research.

When you picture a scientist who goes on expeditions to the Himalayan ranges, you conjure up the picture of a well-built man stomping through the forest, adventure gleaming in his eyes. In a million years you wouldn't expect me, a small-built, soft-spoken young woman from a village in Sikkim. When I tell people what I do, they usually gape at me and say, 'You? Never!' or 'How do you get the courage to be alone in the jungles?' or 'I could never do this!' I am always amused by their surprise.

Dr Ramakrishnan and Professor Elizabeth Hadly, a biology professor at Stanford University, accompanied me on one of my expeditions. I enjoyed the different perspectives they brought to the project, and of course enjoyed the time spent with them on the field. Professor Hadly wrote an article for *The New York Times* about her treks in the Himalayas. My trip with them made me realize that researchers with experience can look at mundane things and make observations most people don't or can't.

When I started my research, my objective was not to discover a new species. But while working on several samples of pikas, I noticed that a few samples from Sikkim did not match any other sample reported earlier. So I started looking up taxonomy, and realized that I had just identified a new species! I was delighted. After six years of diligent work in the Himalayan ranges, our team had discovered that the most commonly found pika in Sikkim is actually a distinct species! I didn't think it was a big deal until people started calling me and scientific journals started reaching out to me for interviews. Vijay Raghavan, principal scientific adviser to the government, shared the news on his Facebook page. Suddenly, people started recognizing me in scientific circles.

A new species of pika will not have a direct impact on people's lives. Yet, our study probably made a big impact because we showed that one of the most commonly found species had never been studied in so much detail. There are potentially many other undiscovered species in nature which haven't been researched yet. Like most people I knew while growing up in Sikkim, I didn't have a burning desire to change the world. I was just a simple mountain girl who was happy to go to school, happy to get the chance to study biology in college and grateful to show up at work every day so I could do my job to the best of my ability.

My mother is proud of my achievement. When news of the discovery broke, people from our town were thrilled. Now, whenever I go home for Diwali or Dussehra, they come and meet me and present me with the traditional khada – a shawl given to people one respects. Some people even give me money. Earlier, they used to ask me about marriage and question why I am still single. Now they only ask me about my work.

When I started working I thought I was not cut out for fieldwork. I debunked the myths I had about myself. The popular belief in the prevailing culture is that girls can do only a certain type of job. The most recommended ones, even to me when I completed school, were medicine, nursing, law or, the favourite one, teaching. These jobs aren't bad, small or uninteresting, but there are other options too. If you are interested or passionate about something, go for it. The world can be your oyster if you allow it. Do you want to know why a plant flowers only in one season and not in another? Go study it! You will be surprised to know that many scientists study phenomena like that. If you're interested in why mosquitoes are overpopulating your village in the summers, go find out! Maybe you will contribute to research on mosquito-borne diseases. My advice to girls or to anyone else is to fearlessly follow your interests. It's the only way to be happy.

10

Casting Director: Shoumie Mukherjee

The female–male ratio of behind-the-scenes Bollywood staff is 1:6.2[17]

When I was a child I'd often hurl myself at our television set. Why? – you might ask. Because I believed that real people lived inside our television set and I wanted to meet them! My mother often explained to me how the television worked, but I wasn't convinced. Cathode ray tubes? Antenna? Bah! Much to my mother's dismay, I'd disregard her sermon and try to jump into the television anyway.

The movie bug bit me when I was very young. I took actors and their roles very seriously. If I saw an actor die in a movie, I would become terribly sad. Of course, I'd be utterly confused and shocked when I saw the same actor in another movie or serial! I felt cheated. It took me a long time to separate fantasy from reality.

For someone like me who was born to a State Bank of India employee, the entertainment industry was not an expected career choice. I was born and raised in Jabalpur – a city that places great emphasis on culture. Everyone in my school did more than just study. One of my earliest memories is of watching theatre with my parents. We would watch a play every weekend. Plays were not an expensive affair and were accessible to everyone. My elder sister pursued sport and I went to music school, even though my father was keen that I follow in my sister's footsteps. My parents disagreed and fought often, but there's one thing they both agreed on unconditionally – whatever we did, they urged us to do it sincerely and give it 100 per cent.

After school, I wanted to leave Jabalpur to go to college in a big city. My parents couldn't afford that and I couldn't get a loan, so I had no choice but to study in my home town. My father had quit his job at the bank and had started an outdoor advertising business, and he suffered a major financial setback in the process. Due to non-repayment of debts, the bank auctioned and sold our apartment, and we had to move into a much smaller, rented place. There is a strong feeling of societal shame associated with losing your house. I hated moving out of the home where my sister and I grew up and which was the place of so many shared memories. Everybody knew us and we knew everybody in that locality. It was my place of comfort.

Our new landlord would keep a close watch on me. Every now and then he would check in with my mother, warning her about me. 'Your daughter has a lot of friends, including boys. You should keep an eye on her. She is spoilt. Nice girls don't hang out with boys,' he'd say to her. My parents never had a problem with my having friends, whether they were boys or girls. Today I am an independent young woman who lives in Mumbai, and I don't owe anyone an answer to anything. However, every time I have friends over for a party, I still, strangely enough, remember the old man's words. Am I not a nice girl? Am I really spoilt? Should I feel guilty for having fun? It's silly, but I am still haunted by his ghost.

Our financial situation slid from bad to worse. At one point I remember my mother adding a lot of water to our curries and dals so that it would feed us all. To add to our tragedy, my father took to alcohol and my parents started fighting incessantly. Their marriage went downhill from there on.

Oddly, as my father's business sank my mother's life began to blossom. She started working when she was forty years old. At first, she joined an NGO which supported small- and medium-scale women entrepreneurs in developing their business. Gradually, she rose to management rank. In 2015, she started her own NGO, called Pink Pulp Foundation, that boosts women-led businesses in Madhya Pradesh. My mother has travelled extensively for her work. She has seen most of Asia and Europe. She represents Indian women artisans across these international regions at fairs and exhibitions. Instead of being devastated by the financial crisis we faced, my mother picked herself up and made something of herself. She is a true role model for me and my sister. Today, if I am ever in a crisis, I ask myself, what would my mother do? And usually I'll have my answer.

After I finished my undergraduate studies, I was

utterly desperate to get out of Jabalpur. I had my television dreams to pursue. I grew older, but the desire to jump into a television never faded! I was dying to get to Mumbai. Many Indian parents worry if their children wish to join the entertainment industry because it's cut-throat, hard to break into, and involves great pressure, especially for women. Fortunately, one of our relatives worked in media, and as a result my parents had a more realistic picture about the industry.

I applied to Symbiosis in Pune for media studies. I didn't want to burden my parents financially so I applied for a loan, and this time it was approved. Finally, I was going to step out into the big bad world.

My time in Pune was an eye-opener. I met people from various backgrounds and cultures for the first time. I was shocked to see women smoke in public; and I didn't even know what marijuana was. When I asked my friends what it was, they burst out laughing! But besides the fun and games, a new world opened to me in terms of cinema. In Jabalpur I'd only watched the latest Hindi movies. I now had access to some fantastic old Hindi and world cinema. I worked hard and thrived.

Zee hired me during the campus placements. I was thrilled because I needed a job, and fast. I had a loan to pay off, and I had to move to Mumbai, which meant more expenses. My job at Zee was to schedule television shows for one of their channels. If a show was scheduled for thirty minutes, it was up to me to figure out when to cut the show for ads and on what note to end it so audiences would come back the next day to watch it again. I also edited and produced a Bollywood news segment, a celebrity talk show and a films and box-office talk show.

Working in television is brutal. You have to be on your toes always. But I have a strong work ethic, which was instilled in me by my mother. My mother was a tough boss when I was interning with her at her NGO. Her mantras to me were: always return work calls, don't leave any communication hanging and always do what you say you will do. She taught me the value of communication and professional correspondence. When I joined Zee she was elated. She told me why she had been hard on me – to prepare me for the real world. And I'm forever grateful for her lessons.

There were many things I learnt about myself in those first few years in Mumbai. I learnt that I genuinely loved movies. I watched every movie that was released, including all the C- and D-grade films. I also learnt that I wasn't star-struck by celebrities. When I finally programmed a talk show featuring many film stars, I had to deal with many celebrities. I had expected myself to go bonkers when I first met them, but strangely I didn't. I may respect them, but I don't have any illusions about them. They are normal people, just like you and me, and I am aware of that. And that's an important quality to have if you want to rise in the film business.

I was blown away when I watched Anurag Kashyap's *Gangs of Wasseypur*. For the first time, I realized what a good cast can do for a movie. Suddenly, I clearly understood what I wanted to do – I wanted to be a casting director. I've never had that kind of clarity about anything before, and thus began the pursuit that would change my life completely.

While I was programming a show for Zee, I met an extremely talented casting director named Mukesh Chhabra, who was just setting up his own casting company. As it turned out, Mukesh had worked with Anurag Kashyap on *Gangs of Wasseypur*. I reached out to him because I desperately wanted a job at his casting company. He met me and offered me a position, but without any formal letter. Even though this may sound insane to people in other industries, this is common practice in Bollywood. So I left my well-paying job at Zee on a salary cut and a job based on a verbal commitment!

When I told my sister what I'd done, she freaked out. And when she found out that I didn't have a plan B, she panicked. How could I be so careless? Did I not possess an iota of common sense? She badgered me with questions. Imagine my plight when I called Mukesh the next day to tell him I could begin work, only to find his phone was unreachable. This continued for a few days. I knew I was in trouble.

Two and a half months later, there was still no word from Mukesh. I gave up on him and began to think about other jobs. And then, out of the blue, I got a call from him. He'd been travelling on an assignment and couldn't take any calls. My sister was more relieved than I was!

Mukesh's casting company consisted of five men,

and now me, who worked out of a single-room office in Mumbai. I was getting paid only Rs 15,000 a month, which buys you nothing in Mumbai. But my conviction to be a casting director was so strong that I was willing to risk everything. I knew in my gut that I was on to something big.

I didn't know anything about casting when I joined the firm. I began by assisting others – observing them, taking notes, and learning. The first two projects I assisted on were *Masaan* and *Bhoothnath Returns*. Through sincerity and hard work, I eventually got individual projects to work on. I worked on films such as *Madaari, Haider, Bajrangi Bhaijaan, Tubelight, Badlapur, Bareilly Ki Barfi, Dangal and Veere Di Wedding*. Casting for a movie like *Bareilly Ki Barfi* is difficult because you have to find people who are willing and committed to learning an entirely new diction. I love casting for movies that need people from Tier 2 and Tier 3 cities. I feel they are my people!

Haider is a film close to my heart because it marked a turning point in my career. It was also my first individual project. It was the first time I travelled to Kashmir too. We spent two months looking for the cast for *Haider*. It's tricky casting for movies like *Haider*, because when the lead actor and actress are not originally from the location, everyone else in the movie must be local to give the film an authentic touch. For example, in *Haider*, a small scene showing a bunch of people standing at a tea stall comprised only Kashmiris and finding the perfect cast members was a long and painstaking affair. I was thrilled with the film's success. After *Haider* I never had to worry about money again. I began to get paid well and was recognized by everyone at the firm for my efforts.

Each director I've worked with is different. Anurag Kashyap is impulsive and improvises on the spot. For example, it's not uncommon for him to add lines to the script on the spot. The actors need to be receptive to his impulsiveness. Whereas for Kabir Khan the script is the bible. He won't change a thing. As a casting director I need to think deeply about my director's needs and recruit actors accordingly. There are times when a casting director will have to butt heads with the director if required. If a character is described as a fat person and a casting director doesn't see why the character needs to be fat, you can question his or her choice. But I must be honest; it took me a couple of years to muster up the confidence to do so.

For Salman Khan's blockbuster, *Bajrangi Bhaijaan* (2015), we were tasked with finding the little girl who plays the Pakistani kid in the film. In 2014 we conducted India-wide auditions for the actor. Five months and no luck. So my colleague and I decided to go to Kashmir in September that year. It was the year, right when we were there conducting the auditions, that Kashmir was devastated by floods. The hotel staff advised us to remain indoors because the situation outside was dangerous. My colleague and I didn't comprehend the gravity of the situation at the time. We ordered a ton of food and stayed in. The electricity was cut off, so we were stranded without television, Internet and soon, our phones too.

That evening the hotel staff informed us that the water levels may rise any time. We didn't believe them. We thought things would get better, not worse. The next day, we woke up to loud noises outside. When I opened the window, we saw that the hotel was submerged up to the second floor. My colleague and I panicked.

It was only when the army rescue boats evacuated us from the hotel that I realized the full extent of the devastation. There were streets with hospitals and buildings that were completely under water. At the rescue camp, a temple, there were 20,000 people crammed in, waiting for help. There was no food, medical aid, blankets or any protection from the brutal cold. Everyone was waiting for a miracle. We moved from one such rescue camp to another, hoping our turn for the rescue choppers would come. Our singular focus every day was to get through the night and see light the next day. As the days passed the situation grew even more desperate. For the first time I witnessed the human instinct for survival take over. The mood in the camps was angry and restless. And rightfully so. If you throw twenty-five packets of food at 20,000 people, they are going to fight like animals for it. In one of the camps I saw a twenty-something woman helplessly walking around with her dead baby. It was horrific.

A week later, a rescue chopper took us to Delhi. Even though I went back to work soon after that, I experienced severe trauma that lasted a few months. I would find myself going completely numb, staring at random things without any purpose. My sister once asked me to turn on the AC, but I could not immediately register what an AC was. My doctor assured me that this was due to the shock I had been through and my lack of access to vital nutrients during that time. He said I would be all right in a few days.

The funny part is that we ultimately found the perfect girl for the role in Delhi! All that pain and trauma for nothing. If you watch *Bajrangi Bhaijaan* you'll never know what we had to go through to recruit that little kid. Sometimes it takes getting stuck in a flood to make a good movie.

Mukesh's firm has now grown to fifty people and they cast for some of the best Bollywood movies. I am thrilled to have been a part of their growth story and to have taken the leap, back when I was just starting my career. I have worked on seventeen films and fifteen commercials with Mukesh, and have hosted a theatre festival twice. I write short films in my free time, and some day I want to venture into directing and producing films.

I have learned that dreams will come true with persistence. I am still the kid that wants to jump into the television set at every single chance I get.

Working in Bollywood comes with its own unique challenges. I have braved the countless relatives who want autographs from their favourite stars. Some of them want to be taken to shoot locations. I don't entertain such requests from anybody, including my own family. If I start doing so, then I know I am not doing my job any more.

Casting Director: Shoumie Mukherjee

I am fascinated by the kind of questions people ask me about Bollywood. They never ask me about how hard the stars work or why a star is successful. It's always about the gossip, affairs, or something negative.

In Bollywood it takes a woman much longer to win recognition and respect than it does for a man. I recently met a hotshot producer. I was with two of my male colleagues. The producer looked at me and said, 'You are here to take the minutes of the meeting, right?' I was shocked, but even before I could respond to his comment my colleagues backed me, telling him I was a highly experienced professional in this industry. The industry is definitely sexist, sometimes overtly and at other times covertly.

The way some producers and directors talk about women is appalling. 'I can throw money at her. Why won't she do what I want her to do?' 'She's become fat. She is old and only has two more years left in her.' The emphasis is only on physical appearance and age when it comes to female actors. Whereas a male actor's age has never been a problem in this industry. Hero-centric movies are the primary money makers. Female-centric roles are few and far between. I can count the number of Bollywood female directors on my fingers.

If girls grow up watching women as sidekicks and in objectified roles, then it subconsciously impacts how they view themselves. It's imperative for us women to come together and work on female-oriented scripts and give women the screen time they deserve. We need more female directors and more female-oriented storytelling. The commercial success of movies such as *Queen*, *Piku*, *Tanu Weds Manu*, *Raazi* and *Hichki*, among others, proves to us that the audience is looking for a good story and not just another action-hero flick.

I met my husband, Tushar, in high school. He and I were best friends. We never dated when we were in school or college, and we had each been seeing other people all the while. It's only after both of us moved to Mumbai for work that it occurred to us that perhaps we should date. When I eventually told my parents about Tushar it was no surprise to them. They said they'd known it would happen all along, even before I did! Tushar works in music in the film industry. Our schedules are hectic, but it's easier for us to understand what the film and television industry demands from us and what it takes to make it here. As a result we are supportive of each other.

My advice to women entering Bollywood or the workforce in general is to not be afraid to speak your mind. That's the only way – you stand up for yourself and earn your respect. Don't be intimidated by anybody. You don't have to please everyone all the time. If you have an idea or a thought, then put it out there for the world to see. Women also tend to stick around in bad jobs longer than men do. Be willing to quit jobs that are not working for you. You will always find a new job if you are skilled and are willing to work hard. Oprah Winfrey had to quit a job she didn't like before she went on to become the media mogul that she is today!

11

Actress: Shweta Tripathi

Best actress at IFFLA for her first feature film[18]

When I was growing up nobody thought I would become an actor. Why would they? The idea hadn't crossed my own mind. And if you are born to an IAS officer, everyone around you assumes that you too will follow in your parent's footsteps. For the longest time, even I believed that IAS was the path I would pursue. But little did I know that life had other things planned for me.

I spent most of my childhood in Delhi. My parents are both culturally inclined, and they would take my sister and me to watch theatre, cinema, and dance performances, both classical and contemporary. So I grew up naturally drawn to the arts. I still remember the first time I went up on stage as part of a play at school. I was just a cloud in the play. My job was to enter the stage from one end and glide across. I was wearing a tutu skirt and didn't have any dialogue. I even have a memory of my mother putting her lipstick on my cheeks while dressing me up for the performance. I felt alive on stage. It was an unforgettable experience. I loved the sound of applause, the way the lights fell on your face, the costumes, the make-up . . .

and every tiny detail. I cherished it all. On that day, I just knew that I wanted more of this. Eventually, I was on stage at each and every school event. Drama classes at school became my favourite activity. Even though I wanted to be on stage every day of my life, I didn't know if I could pursue drama full-time. I continued acting in plays through my school years, without any long-term plan.

After school, I enrolled to study fashion communication at the National Institute of Fashion Technology (NIFT), Delhi. My father always encouraged me to learn new things. I once told him I wanted to learn German, and he took me to Max Mueller Bhavan the very next day. When I announced I was interested in drumming, he immediately found out about drumming kits. He did something similar when he discovered I was serious about my desire to act. 'If you want to do something, you have to learn the skills first,' he would say. My parents taught me to be strategic and methodical about my ambition to act. They encouraged me to take acting classes. So I went to the National School of Drama every single day for a workshop after college. As a teenager with a dream, my parents' support and guidance meant the world to me.

During my final year at NIFT, I came to Mumbai for my degree project at the Times Group. Within a couple of months I secured a full-time job at *Femina* magazine in Mumbai. I was twenty-one when I began as a photo editor at *Femina*, but since I had a strong background in fashion communication, I took on additional work of getting quotes from celebrities and also organizing parties for *Femina*. After my stint at the magazine, I worked for a company that made movie trailers. I think I subconsciously put myself in industries associated with movies so I could learn the ropes.

In Mumbai, I watched a play at Prithvi Theatre called *To the Death of My Own Family*, and it totally changed my life. I was moved by what I saw. I was awestruck by this woman who played multiple roles and carried the entire play on her shoulders. After seeing that play, I knew I had a lot more to do to be able to become an actor. So I started spending more time at Prithvi Theatre. I was auditioning for plays and doing theatre in the evenings after work. When I wasn't acting I would go to Prithvi just to see other plays and learn by watching many fantastic actors. In 2008, a casting director spotted me at Prithvi and invited me to audition for a television series. I wasn't sure I wanted to audition for a television series at the time, but I was excited it was a Disney show catering to a niche audience. When I was offered the role of a teenager, Zenia Khan, in a show called *Kya Mast Hai Life*, I resigned from my full-time corporate job. *Kya Mast Hai Life* needed me to be on the sets six days a week. It wasn't possible to keep a day job if I wanted to do this. The choice was clear – I was going to act. When I told my mother I was quitting my job to do a television show, she was concerned, as any parent would be. She asked me, 'Have you thought through this carefully? Have you considered all the pros and cons?' My parents were worried because this was not an industry where they knew anyone.

Disney ran over a hundred episodes of the show, and even to this day many people spot me in public places and exclaim, 'Look! Zenia Khan!' Even though television was fun, my heart was set on the big screen. As an actor, I want my work to reach out to millions of people; I was looking for a bigger stage. But I didn't know where to even begin looking for a movie gig. I couldn't jump into movies right away because I knew no one from the industry. Theatre and Prithvi were easier for me to enter. After television there was a host of side gigs, advertisements, and hundreds of hours of participation in theatre and assisting directors. I was relentless.

After wrapping up the role of Zenia Khan, I wanted to get out of the mould of this character. Having played a character for such a long time every day of your life, it kind of sticks with you. Her mannerisms become yours. Her thought process becomes yours. I needed to shake myself to the core to come out of that character. So I chose to do an intensive drama programme in Mumbai. Being an actor requires constant reinvention and learning.

Many people think movies are for people who aren't good at academics. It doesn't work that way. In fact, if you are an outsider you need to prepare extensively and put in hours of hard work when compared with the star kids who have all the resources and training at their disposal. They have the right connections and a solid launch pad.

As an outsider you have to work ten times harder than they do to get a break in Bollywood.

Four years ago, I participated in a two-week residency programme at Adishakti in Puducherry, where one of the many things I learned was how to evoke different emotions by breath and voice modulation. I learned how to use breathing techniques to evoke nine different kinds of emotions. For example, all I need to do to feel sorrow is to hold my breath for a long time and breathe out from my mouth. It creates a sense of suffocation, making it easy for me to cry. There are various schools of acting. You have to pick what suits you. As an actor, I cannot have any inhibitions. So I also learned about body confidence through the practice of martial arts. Acting is a physiological transformation. Most aspiring actors don't understand this. They think the gym is the only place of learning for aspiring actors. But acting is not a glamorous career choice. You must have the passion to sustain the hard work that goes into it.

Looking back, I am glad I did those two nine-to-five jobs, because today I'm not afraid of waiting for the kind of movie projects that I want. I know I can make a living even if I don't have an acting gig. This perspective helps me stay sane. Always be equipped with enough skills so that you can work on other projects if there is a lean period in your primary area of interest.

I even produced plays after moving to Mumbai. The first play I produced was called *Cock*. Yes, cock, as in penis! *Cock*, a play by Mike Bartlett, was the story of a gay man who feels conflicted after meeting and falling in love with a woman. Another show that was close to my heart was *Under the Chestnut Tree* – a story of two painters who lived in a war-torn country, and how that environment influenced their work. I took up innumerable projects and opportunities that came my way. Some projects were to pay the bills, and others because I wanted to bring them to life.

Recently I read about a gay man who was raped to 'cure' him of his homosexuality. I was deeply disturbed by this news. I often think about how I can bring about societal change using cinema and theatre. Art is a potent tool to bring about change. In the movie *Masaan*, my character falls in love with a man for who he is, and not for his status, caste or wealth. It's an important message for people in India. As I often say, cinema must mean something. My father joined the civil services because he wanted to leave an impact on society. My reason for pursuing cinema is the same. My father and I have similar aspirations; we just chose different paths to express them.

In 2011, I was an assistant director on the film *Trishna*, which was being produced by Anurag Kashyap. During this phase I was working at Anurag Kashyap's office, and that's where I met Shlok Sharma, the director who would eventually give me my break as a lead actress. In film circles, Shlok is respected for his short films. He has also assisted Anurag Kashyap on his popular movie *Gangs of Wasseypur*. I had heard about Shlok but I didn't know what he looked like. I first met him at Anurag Kashyap's office; he was chilling, sipping his chai. I had no idea that he was the legendary Shlok, the up-and-coming hotshot director from the Anurag Kashyap camp. The day I met Shlok is plastered in my mind like a dramatic movie scene, because that was a life-defining day for me.

A few days later, Shlok asked me if I would like to be a part of his short film. I said yes immediately. After seeing my performance on the sets of his short film, Shlok told me he wanted me to be in his first feature film. I was honoured. I was over the moon. I strongly believe that good work begets good work. In my case, it took me some time to be recognized for my work, but since I had persisted, the opportunities eventually came. The path to getting a Bollywood offer is usually not a straightforward one for outsiders. I did television, ads and theatre; I produced plays and assisted directors. It's important to know that everything you do will add up. You never know when the winning moment will come. To realize your dreams, it's vital to keep at what you're doing, with a single-minded focus on your goal.

Even though I'm a Bollywood outsider, I am choosy about the roles I pick. I recently auditioned for a big-budget commercial film. They told me I was perfect for the role. When I asked them for the complete script, the crew was shocked. I was told: 'Why do you need the complete script? We are giving you the role! Aren't you grateful? You should be thrilled to get an opportunity to work with a production house like ours!' Throughout the discussion, they kept emphasizing how wonderful my character would look in the movie. But, as an artist, I wanted to know what my character thinks and feels. The script is crucial for me. One of the junior assistant directors came up to me and told me, in a highly condescending manner, that I was expecting too much. That was the final straw. I quietly let go of that opportunity. For me, acting is about influencing society. I want my roles to mean something for audiences, not to just look good on screen. I want my work to do the talking.

I once met a director over coffee. He said, 'Shweta is very poised and proper, but the movie character I am looking to cast has to be a bindaas person.' I was shocked by the comment, because he had judged me for a role without an audition. Of course I am not a character in a movie when you meet me outside. If you meet me at a coffee shop, I will be an easy-going thirty-two-year-old. Thankfully, our industry does have sensible directors like Shlok, who cast me as a sixteen-year-old, even though I was ten years older at the time. He believed I was perfect for that role.

I am often asked if being the daughter of an IAS officer made life easier for me. The answer is both yes and no. I may not have been in a position to pursue my Bollywood dreams if I had had to send money home every month to support my family. This gave me the freedom to experiment with my acting career. My responsibility was clearly to fend for myself and go after my dreams. I am grateful for what life has given me. Having said that, life has not been a cakewalk either. It is hard to make a mark in the movie business. My time in Mumbai has included many highs, but there have been many more lows and rejections. Even after the success of movies like *Masaan*, I sometimes have to wait for months without any work because I may not like the scripts that are coming my way. Sometimes, there is no money coming in between projects. Life during those times is stressful because it is so uncertain.

Acting in a controversial movie like *Haraamkhor* changed me. This was my first film, and I was fortunate to get to work with Nawazuddin Siddiqui, who is a great mentor and a kind human being. He could have treated me like a newbie, but Nawaz bhai would always ask me my opinion before we shot a scene together. He truly listens to what you have to say, which gave me the confidence I needed. I have never seen anyone more attentive and curious. He is never bored and is never boring. He has no inhibitions at all, which is very important for an actor. Every scene with Nawaz bhai made me a better actor. I have learned that being around the best makes you give your best. The word in film circles is that Nawaz bhai did a hundred short films for free to hone his craft. Isn't that inspiring? I'd like to emulate his work ethic. When there's a work-related problem, I ask myself, what would Nawaz bhai do?

I am often asked about nepotism in Bollywood, and when I tell people what I think about it they are usually surprised. Nepotism doesn't bother me because that's an aspect you'll encounter in every walk of life. Being human means having biases. Think about it this way – you may be working in medicine, law, a corporation . . . tell me truly, does your boss not favour one employee over another? I would rather focus my energies on what I can control. Nawaz bhai once said to me, '*Talent ko koi hamesha nahin daba sakta.*' You can't suppress true talent. My role models are actors such as Ali Fazal, Richa Chadda, and Radhika Apte, who make things happen for themselves.

Persistence is key in the film business. And, of course, a little bit of madness! My friends have sometimes asked me why I didn't move on to other careers when there were no movie projects in sight. My answer has always remained the same – if you love something deeply, you will stick with it. Acting is my life, and it is going to be my life's work, whether it is in theatre or the movies. My passion for the profession sustains me through the difficult months.

Life as an actor is challenging. Sometimes you have back-to-back projects and you are shooting more than eighteen hours a day, while at other times you have to struggle to find work. As an outsider, I have also learned to ask for what I want. If I am convinced that I am the best person for a certain role, then I am persistent. I reach out to directors shamelessly and make a strong case for myself. You have to be your own advocate. Making a space for yourself in a place like Bollywood means you've got to have thick skin.

Actors usually don't have any set schedules, and that makes their job harder. Recently, I did a short film in which the character was suffering from depression. While shooting this, I chose to live alone at the location because the character lived alone. I did not shower for two weeks. I also did not talk to my boyfriend during this period, even though he wasn't overjoyed about the decision. But I stood my ground because I wanted to be in character. As an actor, I enjoy the high of delving into multiple lives and exploring different personalities.

Movies are humbling, because you are only as good as your last project. It's also not just about good looks and physicality. You have to train mentally too. I've heard that Ranveer Singh once showed up for an audition in character, wearing the appropriate make-up, even before he had the role. That's how much he wanted the job, and that's how far he was willing to go. The emotional aspect of acting is something you must work on at all times. If you are a control freak you can't be in the film industry. It's hard to tell why you get or don't get a role. Many factors play out, and you've got to be able to be at peace with the variables.

I encourage young women to follow their heart, but not to leave their head behind. Even when the going gets tough, I would ask young girls to work their hardest at something they deeply care about rather than follow someone else's dream. Accomplishing your dreams is not going to be an easy task. There will always be days when you want to give up. In those moments, remember that you are not alone. Just think about my story! I came to Bollywood as an outsider. I faced many ups and downs along the way with unflinching optimism and unwavering commitment. And today, people often refer to me as a prominent face of Indian indie cinema. If you work passionately and persistently, there will always be sunshine and happiness at the end of the tunnel.

While it is true that individuals can fight many battles, a supportive environment does wonders for women. Today, my parents read the scripts of the movies I say yes to. I emailed my mother the script of a movie that I just finished shooting for. She read it in two hours and called me back to tell me what she thought about it. I was thrilled. I want my parents to understand me better through the scripts I choose. I encourage all parents to support their girls and provide them an environment of unwavering support. It makes a hell of a difference in their otherwise tough journeys.

As for me, I will face all the challenges in the world so I can do what I love.

12

Radio Jockey: Sucharita Tyagi

Men outnumber women 4:1 in the Indian media industry[19]

Every afternoon while at school, I would be terribly upset because I never wanted to leave for home. I loved and enjoyed the intellectual stimulation of the classroom. To this day, I'm still the same kid who is addicted to learning.

I was raised in a middle-class family in Delhi. Going by the norm I should have been a doctor or engineer. The path to becoming a radio jockey at age nineteen was never laid out for me.

My mother and father grew up with little means. My mother was the youngest among six siblings and the first in her family to get a bachelor's degree. She attended Delhi University, where she was fascinated by the Delhi elite and their lifestyle. So she decided her firstborn would go to the same school where the Delhi elite sent their children. Even before I was born, it was decided that I would go to the prestigious Modern School in Delhi. My mother was obsessed with the idea of sending me there, even though we could not afford it. I changed schools three times; the first two times because my parents moved to new localities in the city, and the third time when I was in class six, when I finally secured admission to Modern School via a need-based scholarship programme. My mother's dream was now fulfilled, and she was beyond happy.

I was young and naive. I thought my life would be sorted if I studied at a posh school like Modern School. While the school was great, my life wasn't. Life never sorts itself out, you see. You have to play an active role in shaping it.

Modern School was a massive cultural shock for me. My previous schools had my kind of people. All the kids spoke in Hindi. Their parents spoke to my parents in Hindi and wore the kind of clothes my parents wore. The Modern School kids spoke only in English. They had fancy cars, expensive watches, hosted crazy house parties and owned all kinds of things that I couldn't even dream of. I saw a Mercedes and a Porsche for the first time in my life. I could never go home and ask my parents for an expensive watch or a PlayStation, because I was acutely aware of our modest means. 'Where the hell have I landed? And who are these people? How do they have so much money?' I often thought to myself. I felt completely left out at school. I wanted to blend in, but my appearance wouldn't let me, and the fact that I couldn't speak fluent English didn't help me either.

My first step was to teach myself how to speak fluent English. Back in those days the Delhi government sponsored mobile libraries that did weekly rounds of the city. Whenever the mobile library turned up in our locality I would load up on books and devour them. Also, every Sunday my mother would take me to Daryaganj, which hosted a big used-books market for the day. We'd always come back with half a dozen new books. Every free minute I had, I read ferociously. I was determined to work on my English and my communication skills. I thought reading extensively was the best way to do that. Since second-hand books were affordable, nothing was going to stop me from reading.

School was cliquey. In the beginning, I was looked down upon. Some girls ganged up against me and ragged me for being different. They never included me in any activities. I would go home to my mother and cry.

'What you lack in money, make up for it in other things,' my mother would say to me. 'You might not have all the fancy things those kids have, but your excellence in academics is your strength and you should continue to focus on it.'

My mother helped me keep my confidence up. My academic distinction was my armour and defence for the longest time. I consistently topped the class in Hindi and Sanskrit, and eventually, to everyone's surprise, even in English. All my weekend trips to Daryaganj had paid off. My father, an engineer by training, helped me with maths, so my maths was always good. I roughed it out to adjust to the Modern School environment, but just when I thought I was beginning to settle into the school, my situation worsened.

Like all good middle-class Indian kids, I enrolled in medical science in class eleven because my parents wanted me to. I had no interest whatsoever in the subject. I just gave into my parents' wishes. 'Your cousin is doing medicine. Many of our relatives have sent their children to medical school. You too should pursue it!' It did not occur to me that I could do something else besides engineering or medicine.

As soon as the classes began, my brain shut down. I wasn't stupid because I'd been a class topper for a long time. I just didn't care about these subjects. I hated medical science and I didn't know what to do with my life. I didn't know whom to reach out to for advice or support. During that time, life was very grim. I was crippled by self-doubt. It was clear to me that I'd succumbed to what was expected of me instead of playing to my strengths. I was depressed during those two years. I caved in and didn't engage with the world. I developed a severe inferiority complex. My self-esteem and self-worth were at rock bottom. I lost my confidence and stopped talking to people. My parents didn't know what to do with me. My biggest regret to this day is my having wasted those two years of my life studying the sciences.

I don't blame my parents either. Literature, arts, history and psychology are not subjects that middle-class kids usually pursued. My parents did not know any better. While I failed chemistry in the board exams, my father's close friend's daughter, who is a doctor now, topped in the exams. She was my competition. It was a traumatic time for us as a family. When I sat for my chemistry exam once again, I had a moment of revelation. I decided that from there on I would make all my life choices myself and that I would also be fully responsible for all the outcomes. I wasn't going do something because somebody else wanted me to. Since then, extreme ownership became my personal mantra and guiding principle.

One good thing came out of those two wasted years: I met my best friend, Nikhila, who now works for the United Nations in Rwanda. I used to spend a lot of time at her house during my two years of depression, and she helped me a great deal. While my parents had difficulty processing what was going on with me and why I had no interest in coursework all of a sudden, Nikhila, on the other hand, could relate to what I was feeling.

An unexpected meeting with Richard Gere changed my life and gave me a new sense of direction.

Modern School offered many extracurricular opportunities to students. They had a programme that gave students Rs 10,000 for a community service project. Nikhila and I, along with a few other classmates, wanted to work on a short film to talk about HIV/AIDS awareness. We found out that Richard Gere was in Delhi, immersed in an HIV/AIDS awareness programme. We wanted to interview him for our school project. Yes, we were very ambitious!

But how does one go about getting an interview with Richard Gere? What we did will surprise you.

We just turned up and asked him!

We wrote a short letter about our project and waited at the hotel where the HIV/AIDS conference was being held. When we spotted him walking down the staircase of the hotel, we approached him and handed him our letter. He read it and said, 'Sure, let the event get over, and we will figure this out.' I could not believe my ears! After the event, Nikhila and I were among the sea of media people rushing in to talk to Gere. When he spotted us he said to the crowd, 'Those girls asked me first, I'll talk to the rest of you after speaking with them.'

The interview went very well, and we submitted our project at school. This event changed something in me. Suddenly, I had been bitten by the media bug. I wanted to be in broadcast media. I wanted to be a journalist. I wanted to be in communications. I wanted to interview cool people. The whole process of chasing Richard Gere, scripting the interview questions and recording our conversation gave me a high I'd never experienced before. Gere might not recollect the scrawny kids who interviewed him, but his kindness changed my life and gave me the confidence to want to pursue journalism. God bless the man!

But the road to journalism wasn't smooth sailing. All hell broke loose at home when I announced that I wasn't going to sit for any medical entrance exams and that I wanted to be a journalist. For months my parents and I did not speak to each other. Finally, my father reluctantly bought the forms for the media entrance exams, paid the application fees and dropped me at the test centre. I respected the fact that he showed up for me even though he disagreed with or couldn't understand my choice. When I secured admission into Guru Gobind Singh Indraprastha University, I was elated. I was finally going to be doing something I truly cared about.

Once again, at college, I began to shine. Communication was my forte. I threw myself into all kinds of extracurriculars. During my college years I met Swati, who was an radio jockey at Red FM. She informed me about openings at Red FM and told me I should give it a shot. I was only nineteen when I auditioned with Red FM, but they liked me and gave me the job. I was an outdoor journalist who communicated with an RJ at the station.

In the mornings I would attend class and in the evenings run to my job. After a few months, one of the RJs had to go off air for a couple of months because he had made politically inappropriate comments. I was on the bus from college to the Red FM office when I got a call from the studio asking if I wanted to do a show. I was petrified, but I knew an opportunity like this was rare. I said yes despite my fear. I needed someone to be by my side when I recorded my first show. Being on air is like being thrown into the deep end of a swimming pool when you cannot swim. You are live to the audience. If you make one mistake, stammer or dilly-dally, you are screwed.

Radio is a tough business. You have to earn your space in the community. Growing up, I played a lot of street cricket. My parents encouraged me to play sports rather than play with dolls. Playing sports on the street had toughened me. When you are doing radio, there are people who will like your work and adore you, and then there are people who will troll you. You have to learn to deal with both types.

Red FM changed my name for the show. The management felt my name was too hard for people to remember. They called me Jia instead. At the time, I was nineteen and didn't care about a name. I was happy to have a show and earn good money. As a few months rolled by, I became extremely comfortable being on air. I was even doing countless voice-over gigs. Radio and journalism were my forte, because I could use those platforms to satiate my hunger for knowledge. I loved being on my toes constantly. As an RJ, I had to educate myself about what was happening in the world, otherwise I couldn't do the job. The pace was exhilarating. People whom I had never interacted with at college knew me by name and wanted to hang out with me. For the first time, I understood what it meant to be the coolest kid on the block. I was on top of the world.

My parents eventually came around. Initially they did not like it that I was working while I was still studying. They could not believe that one could manage both work and study, but as I started to excel both at school and radio, they changed their view. They heard my shows and were proud of me. They finally understood that my decision to not do science and pursue media was not baseless. With time, they learned to trust my choices.

After I graduated I moved to another station, BIG FM, which doubled my pay. But they didn't want me to use my real name either. They wanted to bring in the popular Red FM Jia to their station. Work at BIG FM was gruelling. For two years I commuted forty-six km every day to get to work. Eventually, because of internal politics at office, I quit the job without any backup plan.

For the first time after many hectic years, I was home doing nothing. I applied for a master's programme at St Xavier's College in Mumbai and at Jamia Millia Islamia in Delhi. By now I was sick of Delhi and prayed every day that St Xavier's would work out.

I got into St Xavier's, and as it turned out, my boss at Red FM Delhi was now working in Mumbai at Oye FM. He offered me a job. At this point I was very keen on film because my course at St Xavier's was focused on film studies. I had received a few offers for assistant directorship, but I turned them down because they weren't paying me anything. All these years I'd worked very hard, and I had work experience and a very good education under my belt. Why would I work for free? Also, I had bills to pay!

I ruled out films and took the offer from my ex-boss. I didn't work there for long because I got a better job offer at Radio City in Mumbai. The best part about Radio City was that they didn't want me to change my name. I was finally RJ Sucharita on air. I will never change my name for anyone in the world ever again. I was at Radio City for five years.

My favourite part of my work as an RJ were the celebrity interviews. During my stint at Radio City I interviewed every Bollywood celebrity one can think of, including Amitabh Bachchan, whom I've interviewed several times. Celebrity lives fascinate me. I enjoy peeling away their public layers to reveal who celebrities are as people. People say Priyanka Chopra is stupid. How is she on her way to world domination, then? Sonam Kapoor is another celebrity who is misunderstood. I have done seven interviews with her, and I know that she is an extremely well-read woman. Women are an easy target for ridicule, and as women we should be very aware of that and not fall into the same trap.

My dream of becoming an assistant director immediately after St Xavier's didn't come true. But I was eventually able to satisfy my curiosity for film in other creative ways. I had loved the film critiquing course I did at St Xavier's. So imagine my delight when the well-known author and film critic Anupama Chopra reached out to me to review films for her website, *Film Companion*. Now I host the popular 'Not a Movie Review' videos on *Film Companion*.

It's only when I turned twenty-seven that I started to understand the feminist conscience and the need for gender sensitivity. If I give a Sonakshi Sinha movie a bad review, people tell me that my review was hilarious.

But the same people will kill me if I give *Baahubali* a bad review. But here's the thing: I didn't give *Baahubali* a bad review, because I liked it. When I trashed the film *Sultan*, I was abused and trolled for doing so. You see the trend? If it's a woman, it doesn't matter; bring down a man and you'll have hell to pay. In all of this, subjectivity and critiquing are not considered of any worth.

I have been in radio for over ten years, but my proudest moment has nothing to do with celebrity interviews.

Sometimes, when our listeners come to pick up their prizes or gift vouchers, they ask to meet the RJs. If guests want a tour of the studio, I show them around. Once a visually impaired girl named Nikita came to the studio. She had come by herself. I offered her chai, and we got talking.

She told me how she had been kicked out of her house because she wanted to study while her parents wanted her to get married. For three years she'd been living in a hostel even though her family lives in the same city (Mumbai). She was an ace law student who had been reduced to a hand-to-mouth existence. Sometimes her friends fed her and sometimes her professors would give her money. She had no idea how she was going to pay her fees for the next semester. I was very moved by her determination and drive to study. I asked my boss if I could talk about her story on my show. I broadcasted her interview, asking people for donations. We went door to door collecting cheques and managed to put together Rs 80,000 to fund her education, hostel and canteen fees for the next two years. I tweeted about her too. The tweet went viral. We set up an online crowdfunding campaign and managed to raise Rs 9 lakh in total. This money was going to fund her higher education. Author Vikram Chandra shared the tweet, and the well-known retired judge Markandey Katju reached out to help. Bollywood celebrities Rajkummar Rao and Baba Sehgal called in. Nikita is now interning at a law firm in south Mumbai. A chance encounter with this girl changed my perspective on my role and influence as a brand. We underestimate ourselves and the roles we can play in the larger picture.

Having worked every day for ten years, I finally took some time off to celebrate my twenty-ninth birthday and to allow myself some time for reflection. I travelled to the United States on a month-long vacation. As a child, it had always been a big dream of mine to visit the US, and now I was doing it with my own hard-earned money. It was one of those fulfilling moments in my journey so far.

I don't know what the future holds in store for me, but I'm certain about a few things. I try to use my voice responsibly, and I am going to continue to say yes to things that come my way. I want to keep giving my best to the world and see how I can make a difference in people's lives.

Looking back, being an outcast at Modern School worked in my favour. It forced me to read voraciously, to learn to communicate effectively and work on all the skill sets that are needed to excel as a broadcast journalist.

When life throws hurdles at you, leap at them with all you've got, and you'll be surprised by the results.

My advice to young women is to have clarity on what their unique strengths and skill sets are. Stay true to your strengths. Don't do something because someone else wants you to. Pick a career where you can play to your strengths. And once you do that, work your ass off. Be financially independent. Economic independence gives you the power and freedom to chart your own path without needing anyone's approval.

13

Rock Climber: Gowri Varanashi

First Indian woman to climb the 7b+ grade
French Indian Masala route[20]

As a child I was a slow learner. I found it extremely difficult to follow what the teachers taught at school. I could never get my homework right. I would come back home from school every evening with bruised knuckles and knees because my teachers would beat me for being a slow learner. I felt miserable and worthless. I was just six years old.

Back then, my mother thought there was a problem with me, that I was not putting in enough effort. Over time she realized that I had excellent visual learning skills. I was creative in drawing. She also found out that I had learning challenges. In spelling, I always mixed up my 'd's and 'b's. But instead of giving up on me, my mother was hell bent on giving me the education I deserved. She did extensive research to find a school that was better suited to my needs.

The next year my mother enrolled me at a school called Centre for Learning located in a small village called Varadenahalli, 40 km from Bengaluru. Centre for

Learning was a semi-residential institute, and I stayed back there every alternate night.

The school was not expensive, but it only admitted students based on their parents' commitment to alternative education and learning. There were no more than ten to fifteen students in a class. Every morning the students would take turns in the kitchen to help cook breakfast for everyone. We washed our own dishes and clothes, and cleaned the toilets. We even helped the school build some of their classrooms and painted the new buildings together. We had to be involved in keeping the school functional. This taught us independence at a very young age and equipped us with some invaluable life skills. Apart from regular classwork, the fundamentals of mathematics too were integrated into our cooking and music lessons, and in our stargazing, nature walk, birdwatching, toy-making, gardening, and poetry sessions. And, of course, in our building of physical structures. The school was a blessing for someone like me, giving me the space and time to grow. Many people get their life-altering experiences when they are slightly older, but for me, moving to the Centre for Learning in class two was the greatest gift I ever received.

Sometimes I wonder about the number of kids we lose out to rote learning. The end goal of exams can't solely be marks. It has to be about understanding a subject and enjoying the learning process. The Indian education system focuses purely on marks, and students end up being pressured to excel in exams. Many schools in India expect students to copy down what the teachers write on the class board and reproduce it in their exam papers without questioning it or critically thinking about it. Students are not parrots! I sincerely hope this system will change. Had it not been for the right intervention at the right time, I would probably have failed in school and in life.

My mother grew up in a town called Puttur in Karnataka. Her father was an English professor who espoused liberal values. He understood the value of education and financial independence. He sent all four of his girls to school and college. My father grew up in a small village near Puttur. His family was far more conservative than my mother's. My father moved to Bengaluru to study architecture, which was unheard of in his village at the time. After my parents got married, my mother moved to Bengaluru and started her career as a Kannada lecturer. She continues to teach to this day.

After my younger sister was born, my father decided to quit his job and start his independent consulting firm. It took a decade for my father to establish himself as an independent architect. It didn't occur to me then, but when I think about it now, my parents were quite unconventional for their time. My father was into sustainable architecture way before it became a cool thing. He obsessed about using organic and natural materials in his construction projects. Even at home, he'd call us out if we ever forgot to turn off the lights or if he saw us wasting water.

My earliest memory from Bengaluru is of my parents, my sister and I riding on my father's scooter. I used to stand in front as my father rode the vehicle, and my sister would sit on my mother's lap. Some of my other fond memories were of going to Puttur to spend time with my grandparents in the summer. My parents would drop us off at Puttur every summer until we turned ten, but after that they just put us on a bus in Bengaluru and our grandparents would pick us up at the Puttur bus stop. My sister and I would run around the farms, pick fresh fruit and swim in the local ponds.

My father was into photography too, and he taught me how to take photographs when I was very young. In a way, my interest in nature and environmental science was aided by my interest in photography. When we went on school excursions, I took photographs of everything I saw. Through the lens of the camera, I began to observe nature intimately. I created a butterfly guidebook for school by photographing many different kinds of butterflies.

By the time I was in high school, I was extremely passionate about animals and the environment. There is an endless list of crazy things I did in those days. I learned extensively about bird identification. I learned how to catch snakes. I borrowed books from libraries to teach myself more about nature, animals and forests. Once I learned something about nature, I never forgot it. My teachers encouraged me to pursue my interests further.

When I was thirteen, two of my seniors were working

on a snake identification project. I was curious about snakes, so I would hang out with them whenever I got a chance to. I learnt how to identify many types of snakes. Around the same time I also learnt how to catch snakes. I educated myself about first-aid procedures and treatments for snakebites. My seniors used to catch snakes and keep them in the lab to make observations. I would always plead with them to let me hold the snake at least once before they released it. By the time I finished school I had extensive knowledge of butterflies, snakes and plants.

I knew exactly what I wanted to do after school. I wanted to pursue environmental studies for my higher education. My teachers too thought it was the right thing for me to do. But I didn't know of any good Indian colleges for such a course. Many colleges didn't offer this course at all, and even if they did, the coursework was poor.

In 2009, when I was in class twelve, I attended a music festival held in the outskirts of Bengaluru, and this was where I met the man who would eventually become my husband. Paul was also into wildlife. He went on wildlife expeditions. Our meeting happened in the most surreal circumstances: the crowd had spotted a snake, so I went to catch it. Paul too had been called for the same reason. He looked at me in disbelief and said, 'You like snakes! And you can catch them?' We instantly hit it off. Growing up, he too had had learning challenges, like me. Paul and I are outdoorsy people. We have many passions in common, especially snakes. The only problem was that

Paul was American, and I was worried that my parents would never accept him.

I had been studying for my SAT around that time and was researching colleges in the United States. Paul helped me with information about which colleges were more likely to give me a scholarship. After meeting Paul, I was even more excited to move to the US, because we wanted to give our relationship a shot. It was a big risk on my part. My parents had met Paul when I began dating him, and gradually they began to like him. My paternal grandparents didn't fully appreciate our plans. 'She will never come back! We are going to lose her to a foreign country!' my grandmother would cry to my mother. My aunts and uncles were concerned and talked to my parents about it. 'She is too young. Have you all thought this through carefully? Will she be okay in a foreign country, in an alien culture?'

Many people ask me how I was so sure about my life decisions at only eighteen. The answer is that my school and my home fostered in me an independent mindset. I have learned that if one stays calm and keeps a clear head, one can overcome any challenge. Since a very young age, I've always done all my work by myself and, as a result, I have always had the skills to make the right decisions for myself. I've had the courage to own up to the consequences of my decisions.

In 2010, I moved to upstate New York to attend a community college. It was far cheaper than pursuing a conventional undergraduate degree. Even though the first few months were overwhelming, I was excited by the change. The new curriculum and education system were far superior to those back home, and soon I excelled at college. Two years later I got a transfer to a good undergraduate school. The US education system really worked for me.

Paul was in his last year of college when I transferred to Bard College in upstate New York. After he graduated, he started taking groups of people on expeditions to Peru. By the time I was in my second year Paul had started a small company that took people on eco-friendly tours to explore Peru. I worked with Paul during my four years of college. It was expensive to come to India during the winter break, so instead I would help Paul with his Peru tours during that time. In a way, Peru is like India – hot and busy. And it was my replacement home.

The expeditions we organize in Peru are rough, because often we survive just on dry rice or fried eggs. Sometimes we have to camp without tents, and at other times we have to camp in heavy rain. We once got attacked by a swarm of bees. In those situations, Paul and I know exactly what to do. We are thoroughly prepared for all calamities.

The tour days in Peru do get crazy. Paul and I pick up the tourist group and take them to a budget hotel for the night. The next morning we take them on a trek into the jungle, where we stay for two weeks. Once we get to the forest area, we acquaint tourists with the jungle landscape. We break for lunch and nap for a bit. In the evenings we take them on a walk. Each day of the expedition is a different experience. Sometimes we take them for a walk in a stream against the current. We introduce them to the kind of species that live in a stream habitat. At other times we go on a night walk so that our group gets to see a few nocturnal animals. We also do fun activities, such as swimming, drinking the local coffee, reading in the forest and fishing with the locals. The water in Peru is muddy and orange in colour because of certain minerals present in it. How then do you fish in such areas? We teach our tour group fun stuff like that, and show them other unusual things in the forest. We also teach them basic camping and survival skills. Our groups consist of no more than ten people. If there are too many it's hard to spot wildlife.

Four years ago, I accidentally discovered climbing. During a trip I organized in Peru, one of the young women in the group saw me climb trees effortlessly. She was fascinated by this and suggested that we go rock climbing together. I fell in love with rock climbing the first time I tried it. Climbing is not a sport like any other. It's both mentally and physically taxing at the same time. From a physicality point of view, you have to use both your upper and lower body strength equally. As a rock climber, even your fingers have to be super strong because often you have to hang on to tiny rock edges with just two of your fingers and nothing else. It's a completely meditative experience. I quickly became good at rock climbing because I had been climbing trees and rocks for over a decade. Earlier I used to only climb indoors, but now I climb outdoors almost on a daily basis. I also began to teach part-time at an indoor climbing gym in my locality in the US.

Climbing outdoors gave me a community of friends and like-minded people who enjoy similar challenges. When you are climbing you have to blindly trust the person who is holding the rope to break your fall in case you have one. You have to trust that person with your life. If there's a mistake, you could fall and injure yourself. The relationship between you and the people you are climbing with is special.

I recently received a grant from the American Alpine Foundation and The North Face; the grant is to encourage climbers to push their limits. I was thrilled when I was selected. I chose to climb a route in Badami in northern Karnataka. I spent ten days in Badami, practising the route. To complete the 20-metre climb, I had to clip the bolts attached to the tiny edges of the rocks to keep moving upwards. These bolts had been attached by an experienced climber before. If I got distracted for even one second, I could fall. I finished the climb clean, which means that I didn't fall even once during the climb. I was told that I was the first Indian woman to climb a route of that difficulty level. There are only a handful of female climbers in India, and I am in touch with most of them. A few weeks after I finished the Badami climb, one of the Indian women climbers I personally know showed up in Badami, climbed exactly the same route and completed it successfully too. I was elated by her success.

My goal is to inspire more women in India to take up rock climbing as a sport. I realized that if women see one woman do something hard, they will line up to do it too. Whenever I come to India in the summer, I organize climbing sessions for kids. I want to work at the sport of climbing and push myself to climb higher and harder grades. I want to show the world that Indian women are strong. I will continue to raise grants that enable me to climb harder routes in the future.

I finished my undergraduate course in 2014. To be honest, it's a challenge to maintain a lifestyle like mine. It comes with its unique problems. I split my time between Peru, India and the United States for work. I have to be okay with uncertainty. I am always looking for part-time jobs that can pay me enough to support myself, pay back my student loan and enable me to continue the outdoor activities I want to do. There is always a trade-off, and one has to be okay with it. Currently I teach at an indoor climbing gym in upstate New York, where I went to college. I organize summer tours to Peru and I also work with an organization that teaches kids from low-income backgrounds immersion in nature. I juggle multiple responsibilities while also seriously engaging in outdoor rock climbing.

Kids these days suffer from a nature deficit disorder as they are always glued to their screens and phones. As part of one of my jobs, I take kids on nature tours. I have seen first-hand how these tours can be a transformative experience for them. People in the US have a misconception that caterpillars are poisonous. So on the tour I pick up a caterpillar and let it crawl on my hand. I see wonder in the children's eyes when they see me do it. Navigating through the wilderness teaches kids confidence and self-awareness. Nature also makes people calmer, kinder, wiser and more creative. These are definitely values we need to inculcate in our children. My long-term goal is to work with children and expose them to nature and outdoor activities. I want to teach them the value of staying connected with nature and how that makes us more human.

I moved to the US to do environmental studies at the age of eighteen. I was dating an American, whom I eventually married. I don't have a 'real' job, but do a host of activities that I have described earlier. I do all kinds of jugaad to pay the bills and cater to my interests at the same time. To most Indians I may seem crazy. I don't prescribe my life choices to anybody. These are my choices and they are right for me. They may not be right for anyone else.

My parents have been supportive of my choices. Every now and then I come across people who can't accept me for who I am. They don't understand why I do what I do. Over time, I have learned to build a mental shield so that my dreams and hopes aren't damaged by societal expectations. No matter what happens, I tell myself, I will keep doing what I love doing.

I would encourage all women to make the choices that are right for them. And once you make those choices, be willing to face the consequences too. Be aware of the trade-offs involved in choosing one path over another. Is my life easy? Absolutely not. Is my life fulfilling? Yes. I would do anything to be in nature, to pursue outdoor climbing and to engage with the outdoors. I was born to do this. I am filled with joy every minute I spend engaging with nature. You must find that certain something that can fill your heart with happiness even when you're down. That's the secret to living well.

14

Classical Dancer: Priyanka Chandrasekhar

Dance prodigy who performed her arangetram at age nine

My mother started me off on dance early, enrolling me at a dance school in Mumbai when I was four. I hated the lessons because I wasn't good at dance initially. I was awkward and would always bungle up the moves. Once back from my lessons I would try very hard to persuade my mother not to send me to dance school, but she never gave up. My teacher once made me stand outside the classroom for not being able to pick up the steps. I was humiliated by that experience. It was clear that I sucked at this, and I never wanted to dance ever again in my life.

When I turned five my father got a job in Delhi, so we moved there. At home we primarily spoke in Tamil, and I didn't know how to read or write Hindi. In Delhi schools, Hindi was a key subject. For school admissions they tested us in English, maths and Hindi. My parents worried about how I would clear the Hindi paper. I answered my entire Hindi paper in English! The school headmistress expected I would leave the answers blank because I didn't understand the language. During the interview she asked me if my parents had given me instructions to answer the questions in English. I said no, I did it because it was the most natural and logical thing to do. Why should I leave an answer sheet blank because I didn't understand a language? I ended up getting admitted into St George's.

My father moved seven jobs while we lived in Delhi, so we shifted homes often, but despite that I continued going to the same school. My father is a chartered accountant, and he worked at several IT companies in their finance departments. My memories of Delhi are primarily about packing and unpacking my things carefully. I was a meticulous child, and I didn't like anyone messing with my personal belongings.

But the thing that suddenly changed in Delhi was my relationship with dance. My mother found a fantastic teacher who was encouraging and patient, and she did wonders for me. From then on I took up dance seriously and began to look forward to my classes every evening. God bless that teacher! My mother also encouraged me to excel at everything I did.

My mother played a huge role in shaping my life. She worked at Union Bank for eighteen years before taking up voluntary retirement. She got me started in dance early because dance had been her dream. She couldn't pursue it because she came from a background of poor means. Her family couldn't afford any extracurriculars. If you see my mother today, you would know right away that she is a wannabe dancer: she dresses like a dancer and always wears a huge tilakam on her forehead. When people see us together they ask if she is my dance teacher, and I think she takes pride in being asked that question!

I did my arangetram – the debut solo performance of a classical dancer – when I was nine. It is an act of proclaiming to the world that the dancer is ready to take on bigger challenges. Unfortunately, these days people think the arangetram is a dancer's first and final performance. It's become an affair for the rich, where people spend whopping amounts of money to put on a show for their friends and family. Arangetram is supposed to be the beginning and not the beginning of the end.

Unlike other parents, my mother accompanied me to my dance classes every day. She was attentive, keeping a watchful eye on my moves. After my class we'd discuss what I could do to improve. My mother knows as much about dance as I do, except that she does not dance. She unknowingly became a coach because she attended so many classes and watched so many performances. She would discuss my progress with my teachers all the time.

My mother was the primary reason why I became so good at classical dance so quickly. It's important to have good teachers and coaches early on, because it's difficult to unlearn an art form like classical dance if your foundation is wrong. My mother made sure I had the best teachers, and she also ensured I made the best of my classes. I started learning Bharatanatyam at five and Kathak at fifteen, and I have never stopped dancing since.

For me, dance was never a hobby; it was always serious

work. The only two things I did growing up were going to school and going to dance class. Many young children I teach today take up dance along with a hundred other classes they are enrolled in alongside. For me, it was not like that. I was fully aware that dance was going to be an integral part of my life.

In fact, when my father moved to Bengaluru in 2002, my parents' top priority was to find me a good dance teacher. They didn't care as much about where I went to school, but my dance teacher had to be great! Even when I was nine years old, I knew I was eventually going to pursue dance full-time. I didn't do many things that normal kids do. I never biked. I still can't. I never went on picnics with school friends because I couldn't miss dance class. I was never lonely or depressed with any of these choices. I was a happy-go-lucky child who loved getting better at the craft she had chosen.

In class twelve, when everyone else around was taking tuitions for competitive exams, I enrolled myself in a dance class to learn Kathak as a beginner. I went on to pick up Kathak faster than others because I had practised Bharatanatyam for over a decade. The last two months of that year, though, I blocked everything else out and studied for the competitive exams. I had to get a degree before I took up dancing full-time!

I chose law for my undergraduate studies at Christ College, because the college was close to home and my dance class. The law course was for five years, and not dancing for those many years was not an option. Yes, law was important, but I wanted to be a better dancer than a lawyer. I always had that clarity.

During the summer break before classes at Christ College began, something amazing happened. I was selected to perform for the reputed Abhinava Dance Company at their shows in the UK. I had never performed to a large audience before, and that too in a foreign country. In fact, I had never travelled abroad. We were there for a month, and we travelled to six places in the UK to perform. This trip gave me the experience of what it meant to be a complete performer for the first time. It was a major leap for me as a dancer. I was involved in the choreography, backstage management, make-up and hair, and lighting – the many aspects that must come together to create a magical dance experience for the audience. The dance company took care of my travel, stay and food expenses, although I don't remember getting paid anything as I was an inexperienced teenage artist. After I came back from the UK, I was an integral part of Abhinava Dance Company all through my college years. I did more than a hundred shows for them while in college. I travelled to Hyderabad, Delhi, Udaipur, Mangaluru, Visakhapatnam, Dharwad, Udupi and Odisha to perform for them. I would attend their rehearsals every day. I never partied or hung out with friends after college. I had to be 100 per cent focused on attending my law classes, studying for my law exams, and I danced for the company during any remaining time I had. It was a tough balancing act.

Classical dance is a form of storytelling. Every dancer plays a role. For example, a very common part for a classical dancer is that of Sita from the Ramayana, who is depicted as the ideal wife. Women are either portrayed as goddesses or villains. But the dancer's role doesn't stop with the stage. In classical dance circles, it is important to be morally upright and conventional. In my experience, I thought I would always be less respected than someone who is married and has children. But not only am I unmarried, I also have a boyfriend. Now, that's a big problem! One of my teachers once told me I was jeopardizing the dance company because I had had two boyfriends already. I didn't know how to react to her comment because it was so bizarre!

My family is an orthodox Brahmin family. If you meet my mother, you'll know in a second that she is a tiger mom. When I was in school my parents were pretty strict. 'Why do you have to watch a movie? Why do you have to attend a New Year's party? Why do you need friends? Why are you on the phone after 9 p.m.?' Initially, I allowed them to dictate what I did, but gradually I began to question them. My parents still taunt me about the one New Year's party I attended when I was in class twelve.

My parents helped me grow in many ways – enrolling me in classical dance, investing in a good education for me, paying for my law school and giving me the freedom to pursue what I wanted. But when I turned twenty, all my accomplishments had suddenly become the feather in my cap that could get me married to a 'suitable boy'.

All the things I did for myself didn't matter any more. When I was in my final year of college, they wanted me to marry a man who was in the United States. My parents thought it was a perfect match, but I didn't want to move to the US. They could never understand why, no matter how much I tried to explain myself to them. Even until recently they would remind me about how I had turned down that marriage proposal! However, today they've changed; they finally see me as an individual who has the ability to think and decide for myself. It's as if my parents also grew up with me!

I won't lie. There are gender biases in my own home. My brother is three years older than me, but he grew up with a different set of rules. My mother hates it if someone smokes. And my brother smokes. But she won't do anything about it because he is a man. According to my parents, my brother is 'settled' when he gets a good job, whereas I am 'settled' only when I get married. My brother is still struggling to find his footing at work, whereas I've accomplished much more with dance and law, but that doesn't matter. I'm expected to get married first.

After finishing my law degree, I got a job with a law firm in Bengaluru. Because I was young and foolish, I thought I could manage both my corporate law job and dance performances, *and* practise dance simultaneously. I thought it was possible to excel at two things at the same time, and for the next two and a half years I would struggle to do that and eventually prove myself wrong.

When I started working, I moved out of my parents'

house and started living as a paying guest. I wanted to experience independence. I worked fifteen to sixteen hours a day. Corporate law is a demanding job, and it was hard to find time to practise my dance. I soon realized that I couldn't pursue dance if I continued to be a lawyer, and I hated the very thought of it.

Around the same time, my mother's health took a hit. I moved back to my parents' place to take care of her. But it was hell being back home. Every day I'd come home only around 11 p.m. from work, and the minute I was in the door my parents would start an argument about why I was refusing to get married. This would go on till 2 a.m. They didn't appreciate my having a boyfriend. I would get very little sleep, but I had to be at work the next day by 8 a.m. I was working through weekends and holidays too. I hated the idea of not performing well at something, so I pushed myself as hard as I could. Of course, this took a toll on me. I was completely out of shape, having gained an extra ten kilos. I had no time for exercise and I couldn't dance. I was depressed about my body and the fact that I couldn't do what I truly loved. I knew I had to weigh my options carefully and make a choice. I did enjoy law, but that enjoyment wasn't a patch on what I felt about dancing. So even though it was a difficult decision, it was quite a simple one too.

When I told my parents that I was going to quit the law firm and start my own dance practice, my father was upset. He felt that I should somehow magically manage both careers. Fortunately, my mother was delighted. She loved the idea that I would now be dancing full-time.

During my time at the law firm I had saved every penny I earned. Subconsciously, I was aware that my parents could, if they decided, pull the plug financially any time because of the whole drama around my not getting married. So I decided to save for a rainy day, and in retrospect it was one of the wisest moves I made. With my savings I could finally start living independently. But there was a lot I needed to do before I could actually get back to work. I had to get fit, reconnect with the dance circles and regain my reputation. I was frightened about it because I had to build myself from scratch.

For the first six months after quitting law, I worked on my fitness. I tried a variety of gyms and workouts while also working on my basic dance form. I reached out to every one of my acquaintances from my earlier days in the dancing circuit. One of my friends had started a dance company, and he allowed me to perform with them. That was the first step to finding my footing in the dance circuit again. It involved a lot of persistence, determination and hard work, but I stuck it out because I had made a commitment to succeed.

After I re-established myself in the dance circuit, I moved out of my parents' house for good. It helped that my mother's health was also better. I rented a small space for myself that I could call my own. It was during this phase that my mother truly saw my grit and determination. She saw me work day and night to make it as a full-time dancer and also make ends meet. She began to understand that I was an individual who could make her own decisions, and not just a young woman who needs to get married. While before she made profiles for me on Bharat Matrimony without telling me, now she's given up on things like that. Now she is proud of me. She never checks my messages on my phone without asking me. She knocks on my door before coming in. These may seem like small things to you, but they are signs that your parents see you as your own person.

Today, I have partnered with a friend and we run a dance school to teach young children classical dance. I also actively perform and seek out performances, both solo or through associations with dance companies. Earning a living just through performances is not possible as the pay is meagre, only a few thousand rupees. You have to teach on the side or do something else to make ends meet. I teach dance to groups of kids and adults every day. Apart from teaching, I also choreograph and practise daily for my own performances and weekend shows. I manage to pay my bills with a lot of difficulty. This is definitely a tough career choice in India, as we have little awareness and appreciation for the performing arts. But even on the bad days I love what I do. I don't regret even for minute quitting a full-time, safe job to pursue dance. I have never been happier.

I take something away from each of my performances, but there is one performance which stands out. In that show I experimented with the Ramayana, a story close to my heart. I was responsible for everything, from the script to the music, from the choreography to the costumes. The performance was for an intimate group. The audience was both moved and uncomfortable, because I had added a twist to the Ramayana. Rama is usually shown as the ever-calm and ever-smiling god. In my performance, I showed Rama as a sad and pining husband, who longed to reunite with his beloved Sita. Traditionally, it is Sita who is portrayed as the devastated and heartbroken wife, but I reversed their roles. In my show, Sita decides not to go back to Rama because she was insulted by him. One of the audience members told me he really enjoyed the show as the purpose of art is to allow people to get out of their comfort zones and explore. That compliment has stayed with me always. I look forward to dancing my way through life and using my dance to change the mindset of people. I want to use classical dance to make audiences think. Why stick to the beaten path and perform the same scripts over and over again when you can experiment? The same sentiment applies to your life too. If you are a young girl reading this, don't be afraid to try something new if your heart so desires it. You'll never know what lies in store for you till you try it.

In 2017, I did more than thirty performances. I enjoy choreography and I would like to start a dance company in the future. I would love to bring in a contemporary twist to classical dance to make it more relevant to the current times. We can't be stuck in the past.

I may have differences with my parents and I don't share their points of view on many things, but I love them for everything they have done for me. Dance was their gift to me, and I am grateful for it. I don't know what I would do if not dance.

I encourage women to make choices based on their own passions and dreams. It is perfectly fine if those choices lead you to a life where you aren't doing what everyone else around you is doing. This is the only way to make yourself count in this world – by following a path that is uniquely yours!

15

Visual Artist: Rhea Gupte

About 18 per cent freelancers in India are women[21]

Most people wonder how my parents let my sister and me pursue such unconventional careers, since they were both from technical backgrounds. My father worked at Tata Power and my mother used to teach children with special needs. My parents wanted me and my older sister to pursue whatever we enjoyed doing. They gave us the opportunity to explore our interests by encouraging us to take up as many hobbies as possible. As a child, I'd compete in inter-school swimming competitions and play sport every evening. I was good at poetry writing and recitation too. The most important career advice I got from my father was to take up something that would make me jump out of bed every morning. Because my mother taught kids with special needs, there was a good chance that their parenting philosophy drew from her work in education.

I grew up fascinated and inspired by Japanese anime. To satiate my curiosity about how to create imaginary worlds, I attended a course in animation and visual editing during my class ten summer vacations. This was the first time I was inspired by the art of creation. For the next one and a half years, I showed up for the two-hour animation class on alternate days before school began.

A new world opened up to me and my sister when my parents bought us a computer. I used the computer in the evenings after school to practise and experiment with various softwares I was learning at the animation classes. My sister had the habit of sketching designs for clothes. My mother would sometimes have those designs tailored for us. Soon, my sister began to learn how to make fashion illustrations. In a way, my early interest in fashion was piqued because of my sister's awareness. We spent numerous hours googling international fashion shows and designers. We read reviews by journalists on couture extensively. I was drawn to couture because it was artistic, and I liked the idea of having an independent point of view.

In class eleven, a friend of mine was interested in pursuing modelling as a career. She nudged me to tag along and audition for a shoot at a L'Oréal salon. I was reluctant at first because I didn't know what my parents would say but she sparked my interest by saying that we could get our hair coloured for free. I had always wanted to get my hair coloured and so it was an easy decision to make. I was sold and jumped at the opportunity. At the salon, I was encouraged to get a professional shoot done as they liked my trial shoot. I didn't mind trying my hand at it, but I needed to ask my parents for their permission. My parents were apprehensive initially because modelling was a completely unknown world for them. However, in the end, they agreed because they trusted me to do the right thing.

I spent most of my free time as a high schooler immersed in fashion and modelling. I never wanted to pursue modelling full-time, but I kept at it for many years because it was a good way to make some pocket money. I studied classes eleven and twelve at St Xavier's College in Mumbai and during my time there, I took up many modelling assignments. I was on Titan print ads, Tata DoCoMo TVCs, and on MTV shows to name a few. Sometimes, I used to make two to three thousand rupees for one day's shoot, and at other times as much as fifty grand! My exposure to fashion journalism via the Internet and modelling gigs paved the way for my interest in Fashion Communication when I had to decide upon my undergraduate degree.

Working and making money early on gave me a strong sense of independence. It is rare to make money as a teenager in India. Back then, I would give most of the money I earned to my parents to invest on my behalf. It was an empowering feeling to be on my own. In our Indian society, children are not encouraged to take up odd jobs while at school whereas in certain western countries it is the norm. Working odd jobs builds character and teaches children work ethics at a young age. I learned to respect money as a teenager because I knew how hard it was to make it. I am glad I stumbled upon part-time modelling gigs while at school.

For undergraduation, I decided to join NIFT in Bengaluru. The experiences I have had while modelling part-time and studying animation aided my learning at NIFT. I knew what a stylist, a photographer, a photo editor, and an assistant director did during a fashion shoot. These are roles you won't fully understand unless you have worked in the industry. I had prior exposure to the skills they were teaching us at NIFT.

I have been fortunate throughout school with the kind of friends I have made. This continued even at NIFT. The peer group at NIFT was wonderful to draw inspiration from. Many of my seniors today are well-established designers in India or they are prominent in styling and fashion photography. We have all grown together and inspired each other. I would spend hours at the library studying. In my free time, I continued to work on modelling gigs to earn pocket money. I value real-world exposure. Educational institutions can only teach you so much; plus they need to update their curriculum to catch up with the shifts in the professional world.

My biggest setback came to me after my first year at NIFT. I was borderline short of attendance and I was asked to repeat a semester even though I had scored well. Due to my own carelessness, I was not aware of the attendance criterion. I was shocked and heartbroken; it didn't make any sense. Up until then, I had always been a winner and excelled at everything I did, but now my bubble had been burst. It shook me to the core. I had to regroup and rethink everything.

My parents were my rock during this phase. Instead of moping about, I owned up to my mistake and I tried to use the year off from college productively. I took up many modelling jobs, which gave me more exposure to the industry. Around the same time, I also took up a few writing jobs for fashion websites and assisted a stylist. These work stints made me grow professionally. If there was one skill I learnt during this phase, it was the ability to think straight and keep calm during tough times.

In 2011, in my third year of college, I started my journey as a blogger. I was inspired by a website called lookbook.nu, where people shared photos of their unique individual styles. At the time, I found lookbook.nu very inspiring because people expressed themselves as they were, and the audience celebrated their individualism. They were just happy to be themselves, comfortable in their skin. I wanted my blog to be something similar and I used it as a vehicle to share my individual style and also as an avenue for creative exploration. Apart from documenting my personal style, I also showcased all my college projects. I also wrote about my learnings and thoughts on the fashion industry. I would sometimes write about my personal reflections. By the fourth year at college, I was blogging almost every day. I would wake up early in the morning and write a blog post before attending classes.

While at NIFT, I also interned at *Grazia*. It gave me

a first-hand view of how magazines work – how different departments, such as editing, shooting, sourcing, styling, etc., work in tandem to create a magazine. While I was fascinated by how the fashion publishing industry worked, I was also itching to do my own thing. Organizations have a set pattern of functioning, and I wanted to explore my ideas independently. I wanted to continue freelancing and see what I could make of my blog. So, I decided not to sit for the job placements that take place in the final year of college. My parents knew that if I put my mind to something, I would do it no matter what. So, they were confident about my decisions.

In 2013, after graduating from NIFT, I moved back to Mumbai where I rented a small apartment in Khar. I continued doing part-time gigs while focusing my energies on growing my blog. The first year after graduation was very difficult, testing my discipline in every possible way. I was doing way too many things. I was freelancing as a fashion stylist, writing for a couple of fashion websites, I was a social media consultant for a jewellery brand, all the while being prolific with my own blog. I was grateful for all the freelance gigs because I did not have to worry about money and could work on my blog guilt-free.

In a way, starting to work early in your life is a blessing. I encourage everyone to pursue several side projects and hobbies during their school and college years. Pick up a skill and work hard at it so you become extremely good at it. It is a very empowering feeling. By the time I graduated college, I learned many useful basic professional skills such as email communication, follow-up with clients, etc., because of my early entrepreneurial career. These skills may seem small to you, but believe me, they are crucial when you do something entrepreneurial.

All career choices come with their unique ups and downs. People who have secure nine-to-five jobs don't worry about money the same way as a freelancer. As a freelancer, yes, I must be aware of where my next gig is coming from, but it also gives me the ability to explore many opportunities. And I get to plan my days the way I want to.

Growing up, I had an organized approach to saving money. I picked up this habit from my grandmother who was highly methodical in her budgeting. She would maintain a diary where she listed all the family expenses and she was careful about where she spent the household income. My grandfather used to work at a bank and he taught my mother too very early on how to operate a bank account and how to balance accounts. So, I learned everything about managing money by observing my grandparents and my mother.

A year after I'd moved back to Mumbai, many fashion brands started reaching out to me, asking to be profiled on my blog. I was taken aback by the flood of requests. My blog was a personal creative endeavour and I never thought for a moment that brands would want to pay me money to create content for them on my own blog. I wanted to give the brand partnerships a shot. Soon I established successful partnerships with several Indian and international brands. I had a few tough learnings along the way. When I started my journey, I was more trusting of people. I assumed that payments would come on time. Sometimes, clients would just increase the scope of work and wouldn't pay me for the extra work I did. Very quickly, I learned to draft better contracts. As a freelancer, you can take control of your work by setting the tone of the contract and communication upfront. Freelancers should demand advance payments. You can stand up for yourself and put your foot down if the other parties are acting unprofessionally. I learned this by trial and error in my own journey.

My year in Mumbai was a roller-coaster ride. It was too much work. I had no time to breathe. At the same time, I also had no complaints. I loved it all. One of my friends had moved to Goa and I decided to visit her. Goa has always been a great holiday destination, but I'd never considered living there. After visiting my friend, I realized that Goa was a lovely place to live in too. It was beautiful, affordable, and close to Mumbai. Given that I was my own boss, I could work from anywhere. Thus, I packed my bags and left for Goa.

A few years into my blogging, I wanted to explore more creative avenues and boost my career. Around the same time, I stumbled upon a documentary called *The True Cost*, which opened my eyes to the negative impact of fast fashion on our world. While the cost of clothing has come down drastically in the past few decades, the price paid by the environment has increased exponentially. Most fast fashion brands make clothes that inevitably end up in landfills which leads to uncontrollable pollution. I was shocked to know that fashion is the second most polluting industry in the world today. The people employed by these companies work in terrible conditions and on meagre salaries. And in a way through my work, I was promoting all these brands. Watching the documentary turned out to be a life-defining moment for me. I became interested in the business of fashion and the more I researched, it became clear to me that I didn't want to be in this bandwagon any more. I decided that I wouldn't do any more promotional content on my blog. I didn't want to be associated with it any more. However, making the decision to move on from professional blogging was tough. In a way, I was uprooting the career I had. I wasn't sure if I would be able to meet my financial requirements eventually, but I had the courage of conviction about my decision. I would have to find a way to figure things out.

After I stopped doing sponsored blogs, I decided to pick up photography. Since I was so closely involved in the process of image making as a stylist and a model in the past, I wanted to have the opportunity to create images all by myself and to have 100 per cent creative control over the output. I decided to learn the skill even though I was intimidated by the camera and all the associated technicalities. I started by taking self-portraits and photos of places I travelled to. I moved on to experimenting by documenting inanimate things such as paint drops or clouds. I didn't want to box myself just in fashion. I would also spend hours manipulating the photos digitally. As a newbie, I made several mistakes and learnt from them. As I began this new journey, my conversation with clients began to change too. Occasionally, I would pitch my fresh vision to clients. Gradually, clients began reaching out to me. Today, I work with brands in a different capacity. I advise fashion brands on their brand positioning and I'm a creative director for their fashion shoots. I work on creating lookbooks for many independent fashion designers. I have many Indian and international clients now. I make it a point to work only with brands that have a strong ethos. And that's a non-negotiable factor.

When I am shooting for clients or for myself, I am meticulous about what I want in a photograph. I start off with understanding the brand/client and what is required. I make detailed storyboards and sketch out ideas in my notebooks. Sometimes, the products are the starting point of inspiration and at other times, it's the location or a colour palette. In many cases, I walk my clients through the concept. Some clients do not want to get involved in the details at all, while others want to know everything. I book models, and make-up and hair artists myself. As a rule, I never have clients on set. I've learned that if you have too many people on set, you never get the product you envisioned. Too many cooks do spoil the broth. Many people sharing opinions and asking questions curtails my freedom and brings down my energy levels.

During the last couple of years, I've been interested in developing my digital art portfolio. I'd take pictures of objects and spend hours manipulating them on my computer. My digital artwork was exhibited for the first time in Mumbai in 2017 and my second exhibit is going to be in Germany in 2018 alongside several talented Indian artists. In both cases, the organizers found my work online. Even though it may seem daunting at the beginning, I would encourage everyone to share their work online. It can open many doors for you. Even as a child, I'd always been passionate about animation and creating imaginary worlds and in a way my life has come full circle because of my recent foray into digital artwork.

I have always been a strong-willed person who does what she wants. My parents recognized and valued that trait. Even as a teenager, they would let me go rock climbing with friends. They allowed me to do things by myself and that's how I became opinionated and self-aware very early. At the same time, I make it a point to learn from bad experiences. When things go wrong, I thoroughly analyse the situation mindfully and vigilantly. Why did it go wrong? What can I do to not make it happen again? I try my best to avoid making the same mistakes. When I feel low, I write extensively in my diary and have long conversations with family and friends, which inevitably makes me feel better. Writing has always been a cathartic process for me. My ability to critically analyse a situation helps me learn from my mistakes.

Another big aspect of being a freelancer is setting healthy boundaries. I am a workaholic, but I've had to learn how to balance work, family and friends, and my health and well-being. As a freelancer, you can push yourself as much as you want. You can take on many projects. There are no limits other than the ones you set for yourself. Even when I am not working, I think about work. I've realized that I have to regularly check in with my health as I travel often. I have to be mindful of my posture as I spend many hours working at my computer. I have an app on my computer that blanks out my screen every twenty-five minutes. This is my break, and I spend it by stretching and spending time away from my screen. You must find or create your own rhythm and make it work. I encourage you to use your time productively, and give whatever you are doing a 100 per cent.

My sister is my role model in the true sense of the word. She has a quiet confidence that is rare. She took a long time to figure out what she wanted to do in life, but as soon as she did, she made tremendous progress. She is a print designer and a botanical artist. I look up to her because I know her struggles and how she has fought them. Role models to me are a personal business. I find it hard to relate to celebrities because I don't get to see their challenges and flaws beneath their projected personalities. We only get to see the highlights of their life. Their personality could be completely different from their work. I'm more inspired by the stories of people who I know.

I don't believe that you have to work on just one thing. My story is about working on multiple things at the same time and balancing it all. Having multiple and complementary skills is especially important today because the pace of change is astronomical. Also, people grow and evolve with time, and your interests may change too. Don't hesitate to taking up or learning new things. Be curious about the world around you. I encourage all women to be receptive to change and their own personal evolution. You can chart your own career trajectory and there is absolutely no need to follow the herd. Take the time to understand yourself, follow your dreams, and be prepared to work very, very hard for them.

Success Mantras

I have summarized a few key takeaways from the book for quick reference. I hope the relatable role models featured in the book will impact your life in a positive and meaningful way. Listed below are some lessons that stand out for us, all of which may be very different from the lessons that stand out for you. I can't wait to see where your careers will take you!

1. **Hustle, hustle, and more hustle:** A perfect career is not necessarily a straight line. It can be messy, with twists and turns. You have to work your way through internships, side-gigs and projects to figure out where you can truly shine, thrive and grow. College is the best time to do this. Don't waste your time during the holidays. Find a project or an internship and get to work. Believe it or not, companies are desperately on the lookout for driven young people to nurture and train. Especially now, with start-ups booming

in India, it's far easier than it has ever been to get a summer job.

2. **Build a network of allies:** Many of the women we have interviewed found job opportunities through friends, or friends of friends. Always keep in touch with a wide network of friends employed across multiple companies and industries. This is easier now than ever before, what with LinkedIn, WhatsApp and Facebook. Turn without hesitation to your network for help when you need it. Don't see this as a burden on others. People love to help others! Show up at meet-ups, industry events, and networking dinners.

3. **Learning is a constant:** As you start working, find time on the weekends and in the evenings and invest your time and money in picking up new skills. Leverage Lynda.com, Coursera, Udacity, MIT Opencourseware and many other such websites are just a click away. Budget time and money every month to upskill yourself constantly in the domain of your choice. The more you learn, the better you perform at your current job, and your next job could be even better than the last one. The Internet is your oyster, learn to use it effectively.

4. **Be financially independent:** Every woman we interviewed talked about what an empowering

experience it has been to have control over their finances. Research shows that being financially independent improves overall well-being for women. Make money and then think about investing it wisely.

5. **Confidence builds over time:** No matter what path you take, you will fail several times before you succeed. Stick to your goals and do not quit. Don't get too disheartened by failure, and learn to move on from failure quickly. Success will eventually come, and confidence too!

6. **Body confidence too builds over time:** Many women we have interviewed said they felt good about themselves when they were doing well professionally and personally. When they excelled at work while being true to their passions, they felt confident, and in turn very comfortable with how they looked. Don't worry too much about how you look or how you dress; focus on excelling at something, focus on mastering a skill, and you will automatically feel good.

7. **Keep a list of your role models:** Looking up to someone and desiring to be like them is one way to propel your ambition. We encourage you to have a list of role models. Probe into their lives, find out what makes them unique – what are their routines, how do they work, what are their hobbies, what do

they read, and how do they spend their time? You can begin your journey by emulating your role models.

8. **Don't just do good work, also promote yourself:** Some of the women we have interviewed are big on promoting and sharing their work through social media channels such as Facebook, LinkedIn, Instagram and Twitter. Do whatever works for you. We encourage you to talk about your work often, and whenever you get a chance. We interviewed some women who found many of their jobs using their Twitter presence. As mentioned earlier, the Internet is your oyster!

9. **Read extensively:** It's not surprising that many of the women we interviewed read extensively. Some are voracious readers of both fiction and non-fiction. Some read trade journals or scientific journals, and kept up with industry newsletters almost on a daily basis. You must do the same.

10. **Work out:** If you are healthy and have the physical stamina, you can put in a lot more into your career and personal life. Some of the women we interviewed have a serious workout (yoga, running, cardio, weight-lifting whatever works!) regimen. Fifty-one per cent of women in India are said to be anaemic, and only a minuscule percentage of women in India today follow any strength-training routine.[22] We encourage you

to change this trend by taking care of your physical health and building your stamina. Being physically fit can boost your career performance.

11. **Pick a supportive spouse or partner:** Many of the women we interviewed couldn't stop gushing about the importance of having a supportive and encouraging partner or spouse. We advise you to look for these qualities before you make your choice of partner. This came out as an important factor for success in most of our interviews.

Even though the numbers in the industry today are minuscule when it comes to women's participation, we know from anecdotal evidence that women can thrive and excel in whatever careers they choose, given supportive environmental and societal conditions. There is no reason why you shouldn't pick a career of your choice only because it's not mainstream for women yet. For example, India leads the world in gender ratio when it comes to female flight commanders. Who would have thought!

The women I have featured in this book are only a tiny fraction of the wonderful young women who exist out there, thriving in their careers. If they can do it, you can do it too! With focus, commitment and determination, I know you will be able to get what you want. Good luck!

Exercise for Readers

Are you uncertain about what career is right for you?

Taking the time to reflect. Writing your thoughts down will help you truly internalize what you have learned from the stories of the women in this book.

1. Of all the women featured in the book, who was the most inspiring for you, and why?

2. What are your key takeaways from the book?

3. Write down your long-term career aspirations.

4. What do you plan to accomplish in the next three years?

5. List the names of three potential mentors/role models within your network who could help you accomplish your goals. Now, hurry up! Make a commitment to reach out to them. Ask them to help you get there faster!

References

1. 'Labor force participation rate, female (% of female population ages 15+) (modeled ILO estimate)', International Labour Organization, ILOSTAT database. Early release of the 2017 ILO Labour Force Estimates and Projections, retrieved in November 2017. https://data.worldbank.org/indicator/SL.TLF.CACT.FE.ZS
2. 'Labor force participation rate, female (% of female population ages 15+) (modeled ILO estimate)', International Labour Organization, ILOSTAT database. Early release of the 2017 ILO Labour Force Estimates and Projections, retrieved in November 2017. https://data.worldbank.org/indicator/SL.TLF.CACT.FE.ZS
3. 'Why Indian women are out of work', 19 September 2017, Subodh Varma, *The Times of India*. https://timesofindia.indiatimes.com/home/sunday-times/why-indian-women-are-out-of-work/articleshow/60713816.cms

4. 'At the current rate, female participation in India's labour force is unlikely to increase', 15 April 2015, Janneke Pieters, World Bank. http://blogs.worldbank.org/developmenttalk/current-rate-female-participation-india-s-labor-force-unlikely-increase
5. 'The power of parity', November 2015, McKinsey Global Institute. https://www.mckinsey.com/featured-insights/employment-and-growth/the-power-of-parity-advancing-womens-equality-in-India
6. According to an article written by Rohini Pande and Charity Troyer Moore in *The New York Times*, all is not doom and gloom. The good news is that when conditions are favourable, Indian women have made significant strides in the workplace. Women head large banks in India. Twelve per cent of the pilots employed by Indian airlines are women. This is a favourable statistic against the worldwide average of 5 per cent.

    'Why aren't India's women working', 23 August 2015, Rohini Pande and Charity Troyer Moore, *The New York Times*. https://www.nytimes.com/2015/08/24/opinion/why-arent-indias-women-working.html?ref=opinion&_r=2
7. 'Sky no bar', 4 May 2018, Shephali Bhatt, *The Economic Times*. https://economictimes.indiatimes.com/industry/transportation/airlines-/-aviation/sky-no-bar-despite-struggle-an-impressive-12-of-

indian-pilots-are-women/articleshow/63151439.cms
Cited source: International Society of Women Airline Pilots, December 2017 survey
8. Ladies First, Netflix Original.
https://www.netflix.com/in/title/80219143
http://ladiesfirstdoc.com/
Cited source: KPMG
9. Estimate provided by neurosurgeon Vasundhara Rangan in an interview
Further reading:
'A life spent in struggles and surgeries', 25 March 2012, R. Sujatha, *The Hindu.* http://www.thehindu.com/news/cities/chennai/a-life-spent-in-struggles-and-surgeries/article2961279.ece
'Women neurosurgeons in a meeting of minds', 27 March 2003, Sharmistha Chatterjee, *The Times of India.* https://timesofindia.indiatimes.com/bombay-times/Women-neurosurgeons-in-a-meeting-of-minds/articleshow/41512490.cms
10. Estimate provided by fitness industry veteran Kaizzad Capadia based on annual enrolments at his academy, K11 Fitness Academy
11. Data sourced from art market intelligence and advisory firm Artery India's website. http://arteryindia.com/top50artists
Further reading:
'There's only one woman among the 20 highest-earning Indian artists', 22 February 2017, Maria Thomas, Quartz India. https://qz.com/916557/

theres-only-one-woman-among-the-top-20-highest-earning-indian-artists/
12. Fact confirmed by Prerna Sharma, assistant professor, Indian Institute of Science
13. 'Sky no bar', 4 May 2018, Shephali Bhatt, *The Economic Times.* https://economictimes.indiatimes.com/industry/transportation/airlines-/-aviation/sky-no-bar-despite-struggle-an-impressive-12-of-indian-pilots-are-women/articleshow/63151439.cms
Cited source: International Society of Women Airline Pilots, December 2017 survey
14. 'In luxury, the female factor', 1 December 2015, Elizabeth Paton, *The New York Times.* https://www.nytimes.com/2015/12/02/fashion/in-luxury-the-female-factor.html
Cited source: Ethics & Boards
15. 'On being a woman photographer', 20 August 2016, She shoots film. https://sheshootsfilm.photography/articles/on-being-a-woman-photographer
Further reading:
'Courageous photographers shed light on their industry's glaring gender disparity', May 2016, Katie Booth, Women in the World. https://womenintheworld.com/2016/04/05/courageous-photographers-shed-light-on-their-industrys-glaring-gender-disparity/
Cited source: World Press Photo Contest, 2015. http://reutersinstitute.politics.ox.ac.uk/sites/default/files/research/files/The%2520State%2520of%2520News%2520Photography.pdf

'Female photographers matter now more than ever', June 2017, Laura Mallonee, Wired. https://www.wired.com/2017/02/heres-female-photographers-matter-now-ever/

16. 'Sharp rise in number of girls opting for science, engineering courses', 16 February 2017, IndiaSpend. https://everylifecounts.ndtv.com/sharp-rise-in-number-of-girls-opting-for-science-engineering-courses-10074
Source: UNESCO science report https://en.unesco.org/sites/default/files/usr15_is_the_gender_gap_narrowing_in_science_and_engineering.pdf

17. 'Gender bias without borders', Geena Davis Institute on Gender in Media. https://seejane.org/wp-content/uploads/gender-bias-without-borders-full-report.pdf

18. '2015 Indian film festival of Los Angeles announces award winners', 13 April 2015. http://www.indianfilmfestival.org/2015-indian-film-festival-of-los-angeles-announces-award-winners/

19. 'Work life balance of women professionals in media industry in India', August 2017, Dr Jayanthi Ramadorai. http://fansconf.a-kon.com/dRuZ33A/wp-content/uploads/2017/08/23-Work-Life-Balance-of-Women-Professionals-in-Media-Industry-in-India.pdf
Source: Study published by UNESCO, UN Women and IFJ in 2015. http://www2.unwomen.org/-/media/field%20office%20eseasia/docs/publications/2015/06/inside-the-news-final-040615.

pdf?la=en&vs=3403
20. 'Gowri Varanashi adds spice to the French Indian Masala in Badami', 21 February 2018, Aditya Pande. http://4play.in/stories/gowri-varanashi-adds-spice-to-the-french-indian-masala-in-badami/
21. '82% freelancers in Indian men, 48% women consider it', 9 January 2018. https://www.business-standard.com/article/news-ians/82-freelancers-in-indian-men-48-women-consider-it-report-118010900711_1.html Study: Insights into freelancers ecosystem by PayPal
22. 2017 Global Nutrition Report. http://www.who.int/nutrition/globalnutritionreport/en/

Further reading:

'India home to 23.4% of world's hungry, 51% women are anemic: UN report', 15 September 2017, Sayantan Bera, Livemint. https://www.livemint.com/Politics/8BBA9K4GHvpSvXR0ps602O/India-home-to-234-of-worlds-hungry-51-women-are-anemic.html

Acknowledgements

First and foremost, I would like to thank my editor, Trisha Bora. I am immensely grateful for her support and encouragement. Trisha took a wild bet on me and my idea, even though this is my first book. Throughout the process, she worked with a commitment and passion that is rare. What I love most about Trisha is that she pushes you, that she tells you the truth. You must be lucky to have Trisha as a partner, mentor and guide in any project! Trisha, Chiki, and the rest of the Juggernaut team are doing wonders for the world of publishing in India, and they deserve a standing ovation for their pioneering work.

I am forever indebted to my long-time adviser, teacher and role model, Vani Kola, for championing this book, even when it was just an idea, and for also writing the foreword. Her support means the world to me. While she is legendary for her critical feedback, what only a handful of lucky people know about her is that she is the epitome of tough love. She is the first person to ask me tough questions, and I love her for that. When she backs you, she does it 100 per cent. What she has achieved, both professionally and personally, is awe-inspiring. She belongs on a pedestal not meant for mere mortals.

I thank Kalaari Capital, YourStory, Samhita.org and Amazon for helping me grow professionally, all in different but equally valuable ways. I thank the Birla Institute of Technology and Science and my beloved BITSian friends for shaping me. My special thanks to Harshita Chouhan and Neha Sharma.

I am indebted to my friend Sonal Bhandari Biyani for being a pillar of strength during the process of writing this book. Sonal endured my long phone calls and helped me cross the roadblocks that came along the way. She is a true partner.

I thank my friends Krupa Adusumilli, Krushi Lekkala, Pragya Saxena, Tara Kola, Thryza Dow and Ramya Ramnath for the heavy lifting they did. I would like to give a shout-out to Muthiah Venkateswaran, Lavanya Ashok, Pooja Gupta, Priya Naik, Mithun, Sangeetha, Rachana Bhide and Lakshmi Pratury for hearing me out and encouraging and advising me along the way.

This book would not have been possible without the support of the wonderful women who came forward and agreed to share their stories. They have all been very candid and generous with their time. Unfortunately, not everybody I interviewed made it to the book, for editorial reasons. I would like to thank every one of them for investing their time in a cause they believed in. We couldn't cover all the professions we wanted to in this book, and we acknowledge there are many other career choices in which women can make a mark.

Each chapter in this book has been written after hours of extensive interviews with the women featured. The stories are written in first-person format to make the storytelling experience personal for our readers. The stories featured here are condensed journeys of the protagonists. The last interview I conducted with each of them was before the beginning of the copy-editing process, and all the data referenced is the information I could find to the best of my efforts prior to this process. Some of the women featured here may eventually move on to pursue different paths, change jobs, change roles and change their career tracks. I wish them all much success in their journeys. Some of the statistics may change with time, and I sincerely hope they change for the better.

I owe everything to my incredible mother and father. They created an environment of unconditional support and encouragement in which they raised me and my sister. They let me go wild with my career choices, even if they sometimes didn't understand what I was doing and why I was doing it. My parents are true role models.

Lastly, I am lucky to be my Thata's granddaughter. He passed away on 14 February 2018. I wish he could have read this book. I know that he would be very proud of me and of everybody else involved in this project. He would have made a thousand phone calls to his friends to tell them about this book. This book is dedicated to him. I miss him every day.

A Note on the Author

Varsha Adusumilli is an entrepreneur at heart. She studied at BITS, Pilani – Goa, and then immersed herself in the world of start-ups. She was instrumental in setting up India's pioneering seed fund called Kstart, which focuses on investing in disruptive technology start-ups. She was also one of the founding team members of YourStory. Varsha lives in Bengaluru and is passionate about women, books, healthcare and start-ups.

THE APP FOR INDIAN READERS

Fresh, original books tailored for mobile and for India. Starting at ₹10.

juggernaut.in

1

CRAFTED FOR MOBILE READING

Thought you would never read a book on mobile? Let us prove you wrong.

juggernaut.in

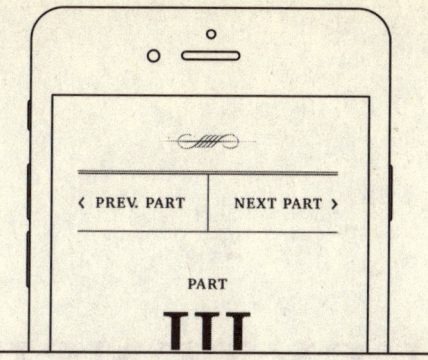

Beautiful Typography

The quality of print transferred to your mobile. Forget ugly PDFs.

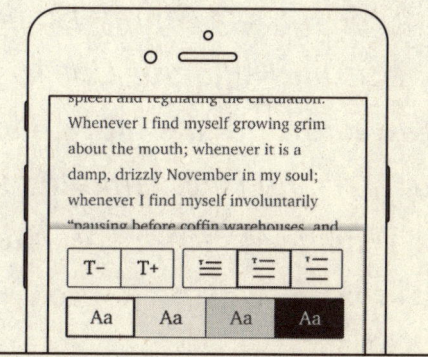

Customizable Reading

Read in the font size, spacing and background of your liking.

juggernaut.in

AN EXTENSIVE LIBRARY

Including fresh, new, original Juggernaut books from the likes of Sunny Leone, Praveen Swami, Husain Haqqani, Umera Ahmed, Rujuta Diwekar and lots more. Plus, books from partner publishers and loads of free classics. Whichever genre you like, there's a book waiting for you.

juggernaut.in

3

DON'T JUST READ; INTERACT

We're changing the reading experience from passive to active.

juggernaut.in

Ask authors questions

Get all your answers from the horse's mouth. Juggernaut authors actually reply to every question they can.

Rate and review

Let everyone know of your favourite reads or critique the finer points of a book – you will be heard in a community of like-minded readers.

Gift books to friends

For a book-lover, there's no nicer gift than a book personally picked. You can even do it anonymously if you like.

Enjoy new book formats

Discover serials released in parts over time, picture books including comics, and story-bundles at discounted rates. And coming soon, audiobooks.

juggernaut.in

4

LOWEST PRICES & ONE-TAP BUYING

Books start at ₹10 with regular discounts and free previews.

juggernaut.in

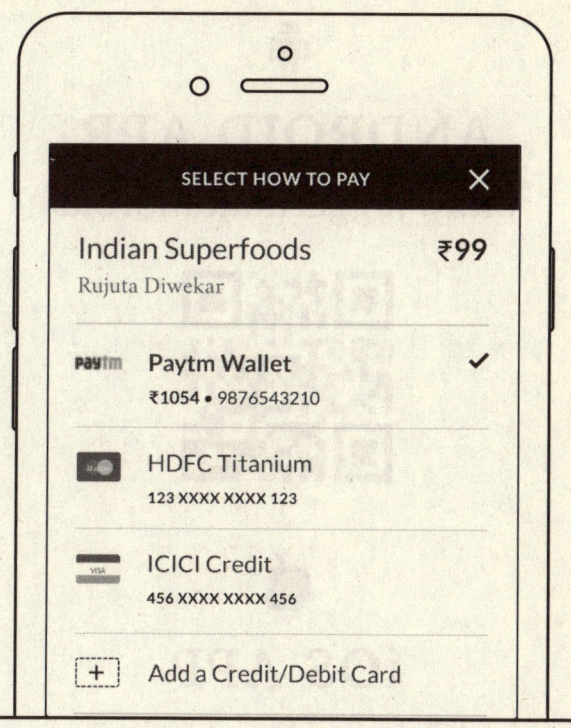

Paytm Wallet, Cards & Apple Payments

On Android, just add a Paytm Wallet once and buy any book with one tap. On iOS, pay with one tap with your iTunes-linked debit/credit card.

Click the QR Code with a QR scanner app or type the link into the Internet browser on your phone to download the app.

ANDROID APP

bit.ly/juggernautandroid

iOS APP

bit.ly/juggernautios

For our complete catalogue, visit www.juggernaut.in
To submit your book, send a synopsis and two sample chapters to books@juggernaut.in
For all other queries, write to contact@juggernaut.in